Other Titles by Dr. Israel Regardie

A Garden of Pomegranates
A Practical Guide to Geomantic Divination - A Small Gem
Attract and Use Healing Energy - A Small Gem
Be Yourself - A Guide to Relaxation and Health
Ceremonial Magic
Dr. Israel Regardie's Definitive Work on Aleister Crowley, The Eye In The Triangle
Healing Energy, Prayer and Relaxation
How To Make and Use Talismans - A Small Gem
Israel Regardie's The Foundations of Practical Magick
My Rosicrucian Adventure
Mysticism, Psychology and Oedipus - A Small Gem
Practical Magick - A Small Gem
Teachers of Fulfillment
The Art and Meaning of Magic - A Small Gem
The Body-Mind Connection, A Path to Well-Being - A Small Gem
The Complete Golden Dawn System of Magic
The Complete Golden Dawn System of Magic Book 1 - Ltd. Edition
The Complete Golden Dawn System of Magic Book 2 - Ltd. Edition
The Complete Golden Dawn System of Magic - The Black Edition
The Eye in the Triangle: An Interpretation of Aleister Crowley
The Golden Dawn Audio CDs, Vol. 1, Vol. 2, and Vol. 3
The Legend of Aleister Crowley
The Magic of Israel Regardie
The Middle Pillar
The Philosopher's Stone
The Portable Complete Golden Dawn System of Magic
The Tree of Life
The Wisdom of Israel Regardie - Vol. I
  Selected Introductions, Prefaces and Forewords
The Wisdom of Israel Regardie - Vol. II
  Selected Essays and Commentaries
The Wisdom of Israel Regardie - Vol. III
  Selected Articles, Introductions, Prefaces and Forewords
What You Should Know About the Golden Dawn
Wilhelm Reich, His Theory And Techniques
Aha! (Dr. Israel Regardie and Aleister Crowley)
Roll Away The Stone/The Herb Dangerous
  (Dr. Israel Regardie and Aleister Crowley)

MANY OF OUR TITLES AVAILABLE ON KINDLE!
Please visit our website at http://www.newfalcon.com

Copyright © 2022 New Falcon Publications

All rights reserved. No part of this book,
in part or in whole, may be reproduced, transmitted,
or utilized, in any form or by any means, electronic or mechanical,
including photocopying, recording, or by any information storage
and retrieval system, without permission in writing
from the publisher, except for brief quotations
in critical articles, books and reviews.

ISBN 13: 978-1-56184-514-9
ISBN 10: 1-56184-514-0

New Falcon Publications First Edition 2022

The paper used in this publication meets the minimum requirements
of the American National Standard for Permanence of
Paper for Printed Library Materials Z39.48-1984

Printed in USA

NEW FALCON PUBLICATIONS
2046 Hillhurst Avenue
Los Angeles, California 90027
www.newfalcon.com
email: info@newfalcon.com

PRACTICAL MAGICK

Qabalistic & Meditative Techniques

SMALL GEMS BY
DR. ISRAEL REGARDIE

NEW FALCON PUBLICATIONS
Los Angeles, California, U.S.A.

CONTENTS

Chapter 1

MEDITATION -
*A Modern Approach to an
Age-old Science and Art*   1

Chapter 2

QABALISTIC PRIMER
*A Layman's Guide to
The Tree of Life*   45

Chapter 3

**THE QABALAH OF
NUMBER AND MEANING**
*An Elementary Manual of
Numerical Procedures*   87

Chapter 1

MEDITATION

*A Modern Approach to an
Age-old Science and Art*

In one of his many books, the late Paul Foster Case, perhaps the greatest of modern authorities on the significance of the traditional Tarot and Qabalah, described one of his old experiences with concentration and meditation. For at least ten long months, he said, he steadfastly practises concentration at last twice daily for about half an hour, without achieving any tangible results whatsoever. He just worked patiently, and continued to work further. Some ten months afterwards, the first results began to show. His labour paid off. He had had the patience and perseverance to keep to a disciplined schedule. Regardless of how dull, tedious and uninspiring such daily practice could be, he proved his dedication to the Great Work.

In reality this is the story of any single person who proposes to gain some degree of master over the processes of his own mind. Innumerable examples could be quoted here to corroborate this dogmatic statement; but one is enough.

More rhetoric has been written on this topic than almost any other I know–with the exception of Magick. Students are misled by innumerable books about 'going into the silence', 'dwelling in the secret place of the Most High', and 'transcendental meditation', and many more grandiloquent phrases. With only a minor exception here and there, few of them emphasize the all-important fact that only discipline and constant practice are the royal factors that lead anywhere in this art. Affirmations about the nature of God and the Graces of God, and an infinite number of metaphysical variations on this theme, without daily practice of concentration, lead ultimately nowhere, regardless of the frequency of the reiterations.

Most students claiming to meditate are merely woolgathering, which is awfully easy, indulging in vague reveries which accomplish next to nothing, save for inducing a 'good feeling' temporarily. But this is neither concentration nor meditation, and is essentially worthless.

Periodically I hear of someone, without any previous technical training, going for several days to a retreat, to spend the greater part of each waking day in prayer and meditation. For the life of me, it is difficult to imagine what goes on in their minds for the sixteen hours supposedly devoted to meditation.

No! I do not really wonder any more. After years of intimate psychological consultation with people from all walks of life and most vocations, it is my considered opinion that most of them have no talent whatsoever for concentration in any but the most superficial manner. A lawyer, accountant, engineer, physician and similar professions have indeed developed some capacity for concentration. The years of study and intellectual preparation for their profession demanded its development. But this mental faculty operates only when functioning in a wide mental set. If their minds are forced to narrow down the broad spectrum of activity to concentrate on a single symbol, for example, at once the mental defect is demonstrable. It is widespread and an integral part of our culture.

TRAINING THE MIND

How people ever discovered the need for concentration, 'to hinder the modifications of the thinking principle', is not difficult to imagine. I suppose while performing their devotions of whatever kind–the devotions of love-making, of praying to their own particular deity, or working at their own appointed task–they must have discovered the natural ease the mind has to wander off at a tangent, and roam all over the universe.

Usually, for the untrained person, only a profound emotion will spontaneously bring about a degree of concentration. And this has to be a most intense feeling, rarely something an individual can produce to order on demand. Love, anger, jealousy and envy are capable of excluding from the mind all thoughts and feelings save that particular one.

Another factor that can produce concentration spontaneously is a very strong physical sensation–regardless of whether it be pleasure or pain. I presume that more or less everyone, at some time or other, has experienced an intense toothache, or a pain somewhere in the body, that has become intense enough to thrust all other considerations to the outside of the mental periphery.

These two factors must be of some vital importance. Ultimately, they can be harnessed to the task of training the mind to concentrate at will and then to meditate.

WHY MEDITATE?

Why should one bother to learn first to concentrate, and then to meditate? Why bother with so difficult a task? This question has to be answered in a variety of different ways, for there are as many answers as there are fundamentally different drives that motivate people.

One person may seek power; another peace and surcease from inner tensions; a third will yearn for love and heightened creativity. All motives are valid. For, in the end, all of these will be seen as facets of one major result. For meditation does result in the acquisition of spiritual power, in peace and joy, and an enhancement of the ability of the self to express itself in love and genius. So the prime motive is to discover and to realize the self.

If you happen to be a Christian, meditation is the ideal way of discovering the Christ within, of bringing the Christchild to birth within one's soul. If you are a Hindu, then by these means one pursues the classical pathway to become aware of Atman, the Universal Self, and its essential identity with Brahman; and the meditation practice will help point the way, if you are a Buddhist, to becoming conscious of the Buddha-nature, the Transcendental Wisdom, the essence of mind that is intrinsically pure.

There are many ways by which this journey of discovery may be made. But concentration and meditation have to be considered within the category of major methods.

THE POWER OF MEDITATION

Concentration is a method that has long been used successfully by some of the greatest spiritual giants that have blessed the burgeoning history of mankind.

The eternally enacted drama is that a man who is actually a nobody goes away, no one knows why or, generally, where. After a lapse of years, he returns to his home town or native country, a changed person. He is enlightened. Something strange and wonderful has happened to him. There is an air of quiet but vigorous authority about him. It is widely recognized that the mantle of inspiration cloaks him. Forthwith he begins to teach a new law, a new doctrine, a new way of approaching the divine mystery–the nature of the inner core of man. This new way promises to bring about joy and the cessation of anxiety and sorrow. It is said that the new way will ally man with the cosmic sources of power and strength and wisdom. It is unequivocally asserted that it is a way for all men, not for a special few, so that all men may attain.

And in so preaching, these hitherto unknown men stir up a hornet's nest and, attracting to themselves hordes of followers and believers, at the same time invite ridicule and severe persecution from established and entrenched authority. One has only to examine superficially the history of Moses, Buddha, Jesus and Mohammed, to name but a few of the great names that first come to mind, to recognize the universality of the dramatic theme. And at the heart of this periodical shake-up of mankind is the practice of concentration and meditation, sometimes known as interior prayer.

Once one has decided that a meditative discipline is essential, there are a few fundamentals that should be observed. I say should rather than *must*, because the emphasis will vary from person to person.

POSTURE

Asians laid great stress on posture as a preliminary requisite. Their textbooks describe the most complex physical manoeuvres in order to find the right kind of meditative posture, and then elaborate fantastic rationalizations as to what happens physically in order to justify them. It is worth remembering that posture of the yoga variety comes easily to the Hindus because these people have assumed these postures naturally all their lives. They have not become addicted to sitting in or on chairs of a dozen different varieties as we have as a part of our daily existence. The lotus position of one form or another is something they have done all their lives without special significance or importance begin attached to it. One has only to watch children at play to realize the magnificence of their muscular flexibility and the ease with which they are able to slide in and out of these otherwise difficult positions. There is only a small percentage of Westerners, Europeans and Americans, for whom the mastery of this posture is a distinct possibility, and for whom it represents no challenge, no major difficulty.

There is really only one rule to follow concerning a meditative position. Patanjali once wrote that that posture that is easy and comfortable is right, and that is the only point that is of significance for us. If you can easily, or perhaps after some little practice, by all means proceed to use it daily as your own personal posture. However, should you not be one of those people (I personally am not, despite years of painful practice) reconcile yourself to sitting upright in a good upholstered chair, so your feet are set comfortably on the floor and your spine rests easily against the back of the chair. If necessary, stuff a small pillow against the chair opposite to the small of your back to prevent you from leaning too far back. The head and neck should be held erect.

Make a point of practising daily, sitting upright, hands folded in lap, for some several minutes, not more than ten at first, without moving a muscle or shifting position. The most important part of this instruction is the *daily* practice.

BODILY AWARENESS

Make a point of letting your mind roam all over the body to become aware of minor discomforts and the locus of muscular tensions. This is most important. Under no circumstances make any effort to separate your mind, your awareness, from these bodily sensations. There is a great temptation to do this, to think of something else to distract one's mind from discomfort. This tendency must be resisted at all costs. The mere fact of watching these muscular and visceral sensations, and observing them in order to separate them into ever more discrete and subtle sensations, will go far towards producing a state of physical relaxation that exceeds anything you can conceive of at this moment. And this is altogether separate from the gains of the process itself–self-realization and integrity of the whole person.

While practising, my suggestion is that the eyes be kept closed. Some schools of meditation, usually the Zen, prefer that the eyes be kept, not fully closed, but half-closed and non-focuses, or with the eyes lowered. The motive for this recommendation is, among other things, usually fear that with his eyes closed, the student may go to sleep. The half-closed position may void this. There is some validity to this, because when the body begins to relax, whether sitting up or lying down, the average student is so unaccustomed to relaxation that the chances are he will slip involuntarily or unwittingly into a deep sleep state. Normally, I do not object to this. My attitude is, first of all, that the ensuing sleep is of very short duration. Second, as one gets used to relaxing in this or any other position, there will be less and less likelihood of sleep developing, and the alert attitude maintained.

The best stance is a condition of almost total bodily relaxation, while at the same time the mind is altogether wide-awake and vigilant. It has been described as being 'braced'. So, the eyes being closed is not by any means a liability, even if the unwanted state of sleep does occur in the opening phases or sessions of practice. Besides, with the eyes closed, innumerable external stimuli are removed that otherwise would interfere with the exploration of the inner world. Other stimuli from far different areas of the psyche are still active, of course, but these are worthy of note and actually, upon observation and examination enlarge the horizons of the psyche.

DOUBTS AND FEARS

If you have a separate room that can be reserved solely for your meditative work, so much the better. The burning of a stick of incense, and lighting a candle, may assist in the production of a devotional mood that may conceivably dispose to working hard. But if there is no extra room available, and if incense cannot be burned nor a candle lighted, do not under any circumstances regard these facts as obstacles nor consider yourself doomed.

This latter attitude usually turns out to be rationalization, a psychic defense mechanism, to protect oneself against the innumerable doubts about one's ability to succeed, or the fear that if one does learn to meditate, nothing will ever come of it. One is required to face oneself with as much honesty as possible.

Here, especially, is the value of a teacher. In so far as he is objective, he can help the student confront his doubts, his dishonesties, and his rationalizations. This confrontation will go far to assist in knuckling down to the hard and serious work of practice. But if there is no teacher available one must handle these problems oneself. In any event, the room and candle and incense have but small value. The larger value is in the daily persistent exercise.

Coupled with this, the student should take advantage of some of the known facts about conditioning. At least one of the practice periods of the day should certainly be arranged to take place at the same hour, every day, without fail. In this manner, both mind and body become accustomed to settling down to the self-imposed discipline by the process of conditioning. Practising at the same hour every day sets up a favorable psychological pattern that predisposes towards success.

THE ETHICAL QUESTION

Authorities on the subject of meditation usually devote some consideration to the subject of ethics and morality. Complex rules of conduct and behaviour are laid down dogmatically, with the assertion that they are as inviolable as the laws of the Medes and Persians. We are told that they are important preliminaries to the work at hand.

In point of fact, it will be discovered that they are of no consequence whatsoever. The only point the student has to observe is that he shall do nothing to disturb his mental and emotional equilibrium. Doing so would only render concentration more difficult. The mind is hard enough to control at best; to engage in questionable activities that have an obsessional effect on the mind, and that will preoccupy one in spite of one's best intentions, is certainly unsound policy.

DISTURBING FACTORS

One can therefore set up certain (arbitrary) rules to facilitate the development of an attitude that will pose as few difficulties as possible. Quarrelling with one's mate is certainly inadvisable. If one must fight, then fight enthusiastically and get it over with so that the mind does not dwell on it for hours afterwards. Above all, the mental debate kind of activity has to be avoided. That is to say, while ruminating or stewing over the results of the quarrel, one may recriminate or condemn oneself for not having answered one remark in a certain way. This is unproductive and unrewarding and should be avoided; at the least verbalize them aloud and have done with them.

There is no sin in having a meal before practice. It should be tried at least once. The realization will develop that it does not conduce to alertness or vigilance or enthusiasm to practice. In this way, one should examine a number of possibilities that are existent in one's environment and daily life, with a view to determining their value or otherwise.

Sex is another topic that for some people may prove to be a disturbing factor to the ease of concentration. I rather agree with Crowley in this respect: that there will be little or no clear thinking on this topic until sex is recognized as a branch of athletics or erotology and not in the least bit related to ethics and morality. Informed common sense, and familiarity with some of the more liberal views held by modern psychologists and sociologists will go far towards handling this subject.

RELIGIOUS DEVOTION

This is another topic raised as being a necessary preliminary to the practice of meditation. But nowadays this is less a necessity than ever it was in years gone by. An agnostic or atheist can practice meditation just as successfully and as effectively as the person who prays for help to God, or who constantly affirms, in true metaphysical fashion, that all distractions are out of harmony with the essential being of God. By pleading for the Grace of God, he believes concentration may be more easily come by. *Religious attitudes are more meaningful and productive as a result of the mystical experience achieved by the practice of meditation than those compulsively assumed before hand as a theoretical aid to meditation.* The practices produce their own mystico-religious results that the agnostic and atheist can benefit by and proceed accordingly. Prior beliefs are in effect worthless, unless accompanied by profound conviction, deep emotion and fervour.

This is not to assume that a genuinely religious person may not sincerely use his faith and his devotions to further his religious practices and concentration. I do not question this sincerity. However, I must confess that I have found it to be relatively rare. The agnostic position may prove more fruitful. Objectivity can be a tremendous asset in this connection.

INTROSPECTION

One of the succeeding stages is introspection. I can only liken this to what is known in psychoanalysis as free association. One simply lets the mind wander. It is like putting a horse out to pasture, without rope or saddle or any other hindrance to block its free movement. In this practice, one rapidly proves for oneself a basic theorem of psychoanalysis, that all thoughts are strictly determined. One discovers soon enough that one can trace all thoughts to a causative chain that extends far back into the past. But this has to be self-discovered.

'Until you know what the mind is doing you cannot control it.' So wrote Swami Vivekananada many years ago, and what he said then is still true.

> Give it the full length of the reins; many hideous thoughts may come into it; you will be astonished that it was possible for you to think such thoughts. But you will find that each day the mind's vagaries are becoming less and less violent, that each day it is becoming calmer. In the first few months you will find that the mind will have a thousand thoughts, later you will find that it is toned down to perhaps seven hundred, and after a few more months it will have fewer and fewer, until at last it will be under perfect control, but we must patiently practice every day. As soon as the steam is turned on the engine must run, and as soon as things are before us we must perceive; so a man, to prove that he is not a machine, must demonstrate that he is under the control of nothing.

USING A TAPE RECORDER

A favorite device of mine at one time was to use a wire recorder during each session of practice. I suggest that the instrument be so prepared that it will run for a full hour without needing any attention from the student. This is not to state that at the beginning any one practice session should run for an hour. On the contrary: it is my contention that practice sessions initially should be relatively short–not more than ten minutes at a time. One could practise once, twice, or even three times a day. As time goes on, and as proficiency is gained, then the time could be extended considerably. But the recorder should be able to handle a full hour's recording in the event of one getting carried away by the process.

Incidentally, on should determine beforehand how long each session should be. If it is for ten minutes, then one could set an alarm clock, or a kitchen timer for that length of time. Once it has sounded off, the practice should be stopped promptly. In this way, one will not be carried away overenthusiastically by recording the associations that occur to one during the practice of introspection.

THE HIDDEN CONTENT OF CONSCIOUSNESS

While sitting upright and motionless in the meditative position, quietly verbalize to the microphone nearby any thought, memory, idea, sensation or feeling that happens to arise. If there is a second practice period during the same day, or if there is some open time available, the recording could be played back so that one may hear audibly what one has been previously thinking.

Usually, the results are shocking as well as illuminating. It will give the student an idea of what lies concealed within his psyche. They are shocking only if one has been wholly honest in overtly verbalizing the stray forbidden thoughts that occasionally float before the inner vision. The development of some mental honesty is a tremendous gain.

Once one has really become aware of the hidden content of consciousness and struggled to come to terms with oneself, the inner conflicts produced by the censorship of the super ego (conscience) is considerably reduced, and so will be the number of 'breaks' in concentration produced by the forcible pressure of these repressed ideational and emotional contents within the psyche.

DRAINING OFF MENTAL ENERGY

The practice of introspection, free association recording, and playback should be pursued for many months until the shock and dismay usually experienced at the hideous thinking one is capable of has been dissipated or reduced to practically zero. Then one is ready to attack the process of concentration directly.

Directly? I think not. The head-on attack of forcing the mind by an act of will to concentrate on a single object or symbol, while admirable in intent, is misguided from the *tactical* point of view. In the end, this kind of tactic results in a shadow-boxing type of reaction. The greater the effort of will to force concentration upon the mind, the greater is the reaction in terms of mind-wandering, plain resistance, and feelings of fatigue and exhaustion.

There are many ways of learning how to concentrate than by trying to bludgeon the mind into obedience, and turning it into a most unwilling and resistant instrument.

One important contribution to the subject of concentration is the demand that we consider the mind as a piece of machinery, intricate and infinitely complex, but a piece of machinery nonetheless. And, as such, it should never be forgotten that machinery requires energy in order to run. Now if it were possible to drain off the energy from this machinery, or to redistribute it in some manner, the machinery would stop running. So far so good.

Now throughout history, this notion having been often considered, various devices have been employed to drain off the energy from the machinery of the mind. Starvation or a restricted diet has been one method. However, this merely ruins the body as such, so that nothing much can be done apart from nursing a sick and malfunctioning physical organism; and in any event, such devices stimulate the mind into tremendous bursts of fantasy about food, banquets and gluttonous debauches so that some of the ancients complained bitterly that they were being tormented by the Devil and all his hosts.

Flagellation has been used to whip the body into submission in the hope that at the same time the mind will also be beaten into submission and give up its incessant wandering. This is a forlorn hope. Usually anyone crass enough to attempt these austerities has a secret or unconscious yen for masochistic indulgence, and the derivation of pleasure in some form from the whipping stimulates the mind into further pleasurable anticipation of repeat performances. No energy is, in fact, drained off.

Hair shirts, abstaining from bathing and so becoming lice-ridden, standing or sitting in one posture for long periods of time and other forms of mortification to give affront to the vanity of the mind yield absolutely nothing. They simply turn the entire process of learning to concentrate into a nightmare and a devilish ordeal.

Depriving the mind of sensory stimuli by solitary confinement is one way of turning off the current, but then one has to be prepared to face the uprush of proprioceptive stimuli from the muscles and organs of the body, and the appearance of hallucinations and unconsciously derived imagery and fantasy. None of this seems, in any way, to rob the mind of its energy. On and on it goes, endlessly perpetuating thoughts and fantasies and memories, all designed, apparently, by a malignant power to interfere with the development of concentration.

Some of the Eastern experts in the process of meditation call attention to the fact that sustained or prolonged meditation will certainly evoke specific hallucinations, which they call *maya*. These hallucinations are nothing but the outcropping and projection of the latent contents of the unconscious. They must be recognized as such otherwise it is said that there is danger to the stability of the psyche.

MANTRAS

Earlier, I made mention of the fact that a strong emotion or a powerful physical sensation will induce a species of concentration spontaneously. There is no draining off of energy, however, but it might be possibly to use the foregoing methods with a third one that will simultaneously induce concentration and circulate the energy away from the mind itself. We have, then, three topics to dilate on: emotion, sensation, and circulation of energy.

Prior to dealing with these three ideas directly, however, there is one more issue to be enlarged on, since it bears indirectly on them. There is, traditionally, a simple device having as its intent the slowing down of the quicksilver-like movement of the mind in all directions at once. It is known as a mantra. Apart from all other considerations, a mantra is simply a word or a phrase, usually of a sacred or religious import, which is repeated over and over again, either audibly or subvocally, but more often mentally, until after some days it is taken up by the mind itself. In that case, it goes on repeating itself automatically. Thus, a mechanical type of concentration is acquired that can then be used to further the pre-determined goal.

There are Eastern mantras and Western affirmations. There is little to choose between them. Only your own preference or prejudice is the crucial factor to be considered. Some of the classical Eastern ones are: *Om Tat Sat! Tat Twam Asi; Om nimaha shivaya om; Om mani padme hum.* Regardless of what their literal meanings may be, they take on another meaning altogether after their repetition has become an automatic process. Insights dawn spontaneously.

Metaphysical mantras, based upon Christianity, are most common: 'The Lord is my Shepherd, I shall not want' has achieved a wide popularity, with some other phrases extrapolated from the Scriptures.

A mantra taken from the Catholic missal is also very effective: *Kyrie eleison. Christe eleison.* This same missal may be used to indicate many more similarly effective ones. The equivalent of one of these phrases from the Russian Orthodox Church *Gospody polmilui* is most euphonious and makes for a good rhythmic mantra. The Eastern Church has a melodious hymn sung on Good Friday consisting only of these two words, sung over and over again in a most effective manner.

'Lord Jesus Christ, Son of God, have mercy on me a poor sinner.' This is a Christian mantra that has been described very poignantly in *The Way of a Pilgrim,* a book every student should read. It is about a simple Russian peasant who wanted to discover the meaning and method of the Biblical injunction 'to pray without ceasing' and 'to pray with the heart'.

I must quote the following passage from the book, for it is so naive, sincere and so technically superb that it cannot help being useful:

> Picture to yourself your heart in just the same way, turn your eyes to it just as though you were looking at it through your breast, and picture it as clearly as you can. And with your ears listen closely to its beating, beat by beat. When you have got into the way of doing this, begin to fit the words of the Prayer to the beats of the heart one after the other, looking at it all the time. Thus, with the first beat, say or think, 'Lord', with the second, 'Jesus', with the third, 'Christ', with the fourth, 'have mercy', and with the fifth, 'on me'. And doit over and over again. This will come easily to you, for you already know the groundwork and the first part of praying with the heart.

In the book, the pilgrim is describing the method to a blind man who had previously become familiar with the Russian mystical classic *The Philokallia*.

> Afterwards, when you have grown used to what I have just told you about, you must begin bringing the whole Prayer of Jesus into and out of your heart in time with your breathing, as the Fathers taught. Thus, as you draw your breath in, say, or imagine yourself saying, 'Lord Jesus Christ', and as you breathe out again, 'have mercy on me'. Do this often and as much as you can, and in a short space of time you will feel a slight and not unpleasant pain in your heart, followed by a warmth. Thus by God's help you will get the joy of self-acting inward prayer of the heart.

Joel Goldsmith gives several of these modern metaphysical affirmations in his excellent book *The Art of Meditation*, which should certainly appear on any list of worthwhile books on the topic of meditation. And of course we must never forget the famous book of Mary Baker Eddy, which became the backbone of the Christian Science Movement. 'God is All in all. God is good. God is mind God, Spirit, being all, nothing is matter.' The whole of this dogmatic statement (or only parts of it) was used as affirmation, with the intent of turning one's mind in an act of concentration to God for the healing of bodily or mental ills and wants. The New Thought movement, which has evolved by devious routes from the mainstream of Christian Science, has likewise devised hundreds of new affirmations. The little magazines published by the Unity organization sometimes give a different affirmation for every day of the week or month, as aids to meditation.

The Mohammedans have a long sonorous Arabic mantra, which for pure euphony has much to recommend it: *Qol; Hua Allahu achad; Allahu Assamad; lam yalid walam yulad; walam yakun lahu kufwan achad.* Translated into English, which has little to do with the efficiency of a mantra, it means: 'Say, He is God alone! God the Eternal! He begets not and is not begotten! Nor is there like unto Him any one!'

Any affirmation or mantra having its roots in ancient magico-religious tradition is 'There is no part of me which is not the Gods.' Originally it was part of one of the rituals in the Egyptian *Book of the Dead*. In the middle of the nineteenth century it was appropriated by the Hermetic Order of the Golden Dawn, one of whose chiefs, MacGregor Mathers, used it as a greeting to whomsoever he met.

Crowley's mantra from *The Book of the Law* also has a sonorous rhythm. He transliterated this from an Egyptian stele in the Baoulak Museum: *A ka dua. Tuf ur biu. Bi aa chefu. Dudu ner af an nuteru.* His poetic rendering of this is given as:

Unity uttermost showed!
I adore the might of Thy breath,
Supreme and terrible God,
Who makes the Gods and Death
To tremble before Thee:–
I, I adore Thee!

One of the famous Buddhist mantras is: *Namo tasso Bhagavato Arahato Samma-sambuddhasa.* Its meaning is: 'Hail unto Thee, the Blessed One, the Perfected One, the Supremely Enlightened One.'

There are many others. It only remains for the student to select the one that he is attracted towards, and for which he feels some sympathy. It really would not matter what its nature was. For example, consider the following: 'Hey diddle diddle. The cat and the fiddle. The cow jumped over the moon.' Were he to feel that he could readily seize upon this prosaic nursery rhyme, repeating it over and over again, it would serve for the student just as effectively as any other mantra.

PRACTICING WITH A MANTRA

Whatever it is, select a mantra that suits you–and then start practising. I suggest that at the outset it be repeated audibly. Only later, as familiarity with the procedure grows, should it be transferred to the psyche to be repeated silently or mentally.

My own predilection is in the area of the Qalabah. A mantra I have often used is *Eheieh*, the divine name attributed to *Kether* the first *Sephirah* or emanation on The Tree of Life. In the past I have often visualized a large Hebrew letter, *Shin*, in bold red outlines above the crown of the head, while continuously vibrating this single word. On other occasions I have used *Achath Ruach Elohim chayim* which means 'One (is she) the Spirit of the Everliving God.' The meaning, however, is subordinate to the continued vibration of the name and to trained the mind to take it up spontaneously. This sounds difficult–as does the whole business of practice in this area. But once one has achieved a steady discipline, it is far less difficult than anticipated. Probably the most difficult part of the entire project is simply to make up one's mind to begin, and then sticking to it. Once this initial resistance is overcome, the mastery of a mantra is, actually, relatively easy.

If the student happens to be a religiously-minded person–regardless of his denomination, which is not particularly important to this issue–the use of a mantra can be infinitely rewarding. The repetition of the phrase–be it from the Psalms, the Gospels, the Koran, the Vedas, or even the *Book of the Dead*–is accompanied by the emergence of a great deal of effect. The sincerely devout Jewish Qabalist who repeats the ancient prayer 'Hear O Israel: the Lord our God, the Lord is One' is investing this sentence with a tremendous amount of energy and emotion. *It is this passion that directs the mind one-pointedly towards the maintenance of the repetition, until concentration is obtained.* And so with the orthodox Catholic who, like the hero of *The Way of the Pilgrim*, repeats fervently 'O Lord Jesus Christ, Son of God, have mercy upon me a poor sinner.' The loading of emotion on to the mechanical repetition of the mantra forces the recalcitrant mind to behave, inducing a deep state of concentration. With practice, the concentration can be turned on and off until it becomes a faculty that is as readily available as is the electric current in the modern home.

MANTRAS FOR ATHEISTS OR AGNOSTICS

The agnostic or atheist who has no religious feeling, *per se*, and who thus will not be emotionally moved by the more conventional religious mantras, can nonetheless still avail himself of the distinct benefits to be obtained by employing emotion as a tool. He could select some phrase from a poem or a novel of any kind that has moved him profoundly–and I am certain this has happened at some time to almost everybody–and then use this as his own mantra. Failing this, he could fall back on some personal private experience, such as the courting of a lover in early adolescent days when emotion ran high. And picturing this lover in mind, he could repeat over and over again, as if it were a religious mantra, 'Darling, I love you! Darling, I love you!' and if this combination of mental picture and repeated phrase can evoke the deep emotion that was felt long years anterior to practice, it will succeed no less than the religiously oriented mantra in developing concentration.

THE FIRST STAGE

'What is meant by holding the mind to certain points?' asks Vivekananda in his excellent book *Raja Yoga*. 'Forcing the mind to feel certain parts of the body to the exclusion of others. For instance, try to feel only the hand, to the exclusion of other parts of the body. When the *Chitta*, or mind-stuff, is confined and limited to a certain place, this is called *Dharana*. This *Dharana* is of various sorts, and along with it, it is better to have a little play of the imagination. For instance, the mind should be made to think of one point in the heart. That is very difficult; an easier way is to image a lotus there. That lotus is full of light, effulgent light. Put the mind there.'

BREATHING

The next stage is to practise simple rhythmic breathing. The simplicity of this method is its great advantage. It consists of inhaling slowly to a certain count, and exhaling to the same count. If one's chest is tight muscularly, then one should be guided accordingly to select a short rhythm (such as 1, and 2, and 3, and 4) and then exhale to the same rhythm. It is my suggestion to include 'and' between every number so as to slow down the counting process. This is most important. For not only does the establishment of the rhythm produce some perceptible physical results, but at the same time the gradual extension of the rhythm results in the slowing down of mental activity. As the muscular tensions are released, longer rhythms may be used.

The development of the rhythm sooner or later sets up well-defined physical sensations, largely of two kinds–though this is not to say that there are not many others. The first is the experiencing of a tingling sensation all over the body. It can easily be likened to that sensation when one has been pressing on a limb and the circulation has been initially cut off for a few seconds. When the pressure is removed, a prickling sensation is experienced as the blood circulation is restored. Rhythmic breathing initiates an analogous sensation in every cell throughout the entire body.

Parallel with this is a peculiar rippling sensation very hard to describe that is experienced in the diaphragmatic segment of the thorax. As it becomes established by persisting with the rhythmic breathing it tends to spread widely, until there is a well-defined feeling of a total bodily pulsation. These have to be experienced to fully appreciate the nature of this description. Finally, these sensations are accompanied by pleasant feelings. Some describe them as 'soft', 'melting', 'delicious'.

These extraordinary and unusual feelings are but the harbingers of the ineffable bliss and ecstasy that, one day, will occur as the later spiritual results unfold. 'The body is weary, and the soul is sore weary, but ever abides the sure consciousness of ecstasy, unknown, yet known in that its being is certain. O Lord, be my helper and bring me to the bliss of the beloved!'

THE POWER OF RHYTHM

The experience of a pleasant emotional response no matter how gentle or light to the rhythmic breathing, will go a long way towards facilitating a state of concentration. With the process eliciting pleasure there will be less tendency for the mind to wander –except to other former experiences when pleasure was the keynote. There is likely to be some mind-wandering on purely pleasurable experience. But however much wandering there is, it represents the beginning of some concentration on one particular topic.

Furthermore, the experience of a definite sensation or a diaphragmatic rippling will be very heartening and encouraging to the beginner. It will comprise another aid to focusing the mind on a single point–in this case, the breathing process itself. Having to count mentally in order to establish the rhythm also conduces to concentration. A mechanical aid in this direction is a metronome. Listening to the loud clicking, and timing one's breathing in coordination with the sound, is a still further aid to concentration.

Nor is this all. It has long been know that mental hyperactivity is somehow tied to respiratory rapidity. If we are mentally disturbed or excited, the breathing tends to become rapid. This would suggest, then, that if we slow down the rate of respiration to an easy rhythmic rate, the mind's furious turbulence follows suit and can be controlled, so that then, after you have become accustomed to breathing to a simple rhythm of, let us say, four in and four out, the rate can be changed to four in and eight out. Again, the word 'and' should be inserted between each number so as to prevent the likelihood of hurry. Above all, strain should be avoided. Here the good sense of the student has to be called upon. If he has a more experienced friend or fellow-student who can act in this instance as an authoritative teacher, he will see that the student does not hurry or strain while striving for a prolonged rhythm.

FASCINATING THE MIND

As skill and ease are obtained, the rhythm can be changed in a variety of ways: first, to prevent boredom, which is an ever-present enemy, and second, because the different sensations engineered by a different rhythm, will have the effect of fixing the mind upon them. In other words, *the sensations themselves facilitate concentration.*

I cannot stress this notion too strongly. In my experience, it is most important and I do not feel that this has been stressed sufficiently by modern authorities who, I am sure, know a good deal more about concentration and meditation than I do. Initially, I obtained the clue from two classical books on Yoga– *The Hatha Yoga Pradipika* and the *Shiva Sanhita*. Both of them describe a whole variety of bizarre practices with which we are not in the least bit concerned. But as I read them, years ago, I noticed a phrase common to both; that when the sounds of the Nada occur (The Voice of the Silence, as Blavatsky put it)–sounds that are internally elicited as certain practices are performed–the mind becomes fascinated by them, being drawn to them irresistibly in much the same way as a bird is irresistibly fascinated by the steady gaze of a snake.

This description stayed with me for many years, until in the course of considerable experimentation with breathing processes–as part of preparation for meditation, and, later, as an operational tool of the Reichian system of psychotherapy–I suddenly joined them together. For I found that these breathing processes, even on a superficial level, without having progressed to the point of eliciting the sounds of the Nada, brought about a variety of somatic and visceral sensations. These kept me utterly fascinated so that wool-gathering was the last thing in the world that could occur. And then, as the years wore on, it occurred to me that this could be used as an operational tool in the development of concentration. In other words, *concentration followed spontaneously and inevitably as the breathing practice produced massive sensory responses.*

EFFECT OF PROLONGED CONCENTRATION

A most interesting phenomenon may be observed as the outcome of this. If, for example, a series of curious tingling and prickling sensations are initiated in the feet, one's attention becomes automatically drawn to that area. Concentration on the feet develops. The first effect of this concentration is that the sensations become, gradually, enormously heightened. The feet feel alive, buzzing, suffused with electrical energy, or so it seems. This may continue for some considerable time.

Now if the concentration persists on that one spot, unwaveringly and steadfastly, then something happens for which one is totally unprepared. The tingling continues–but a sense of numbness in the feet makes its appearance. Gradually, all awareness of the feet fades out entirely. This is altogether paradoxical. The feet feel alive and vital but at the same time there is no direct awareness of feet. In other words, a basic law evolves out of this. If concentration is prolonged, then sensation becomes almost entirely expunged. The feet disappear from consciousness.

If one were concentrating on sensations in the nose, shortly one would have no awareness of nose at all. It would disappear from view altogether. One might have to open one's eyes and look in a mirror, or bring one's hand up to one's face in order to ascertain whether the nose is still there.

A method that bears some resemblance to this is to be found within Zen Buddhism of the Soto sect. It recommends a meditation practice, 'This very body is Buddha.' When persisted in, psychological phenomena occur of the type referred to above, for the awareness of the body disappears to be replaced by another kind of awareness. This, when meditated upon, is also expunged in very much the same way.

DISPLACING THE EGO

This finding is fraught with the most serious and important consequences when treading the Path. It is axiomatic in most branches of mysticism and occultism, that the ego–or the conscious mind, or the cortex of the brain–is the 'dragon in the way'. The mind is the slayer of the Real. Let the disciple slay the slayer.' That is to say, it is the obstacle to realizing that God is here and now, that there is in reality no separation between man and Nature, or between any one soul and the entire universe. This unity has existed from time immemorial and will continue to exist in all time to come. It is only the limitations of our thinking, of our surface consciousness fed by stimuli from the senses, that blind us to the reality of the omnipresence and immanence of God. The 'heresy of separateness' is essentially a product of the ego. It is not a fact in nature.

If therefore the ego can be pushed out of the way by one device or another, then we could become conscious, or we could *realize* as factual, the unity of all of life. In sleep the ego is displaced, but so is the perceiver; in drunkenness the ego is eclipsed–and the perceiver is too; in concentration one disciplines oneself to be able to constrain all thinking to one point–and then ultimately to drop it altogether. In other words, this training is devised so that one can stop thinking, at will, and to resume thinking, when it is necessary to return to one's daily affairs, also at will. When thinking is suspended in this manner, but maintaining vigilance and conscious awareness, then this is enlightenment. God is! It was always thus, and will always be thus. It remained only to get the ego out of the way.

When considering the law of concentration that we are discussing, it becomes clear that if all the attention were concentrated upon the ego itself, at first such an ego-awareness might be extraordinarily heightened. It would appear as if one had a hypertrophied ego, an egomania. But were the concentration to be prolonged, then gradually this egomania would subside and eventually fade out of view entirely. It would leave only an actively empty mind–paradox that this may seem to be–that is acutely conscious of being at one with God and Love and Life and Beauty.

If we must give names to the goals of The Great Work, the development of concentration and meditation, then we have them here: to become acutely aware of one's essential identity with the roo and source of life itself, and to become a conscious agent for its continuous activity. Egotism rooted in the self becomes universally enlarged to include the Self of All, because That is All there is. Meditation on the Hindu mantra will disclose this to be the meaning of *Tat Tvam Asi*.

To arrive at this exalted mystical consciousness, which is the goal of all systems of enlightenment, Eastern or Western, we have to become adepts in the utilization of concentration and meditation. And this is why we are discussing ways and means of developing techniques that lead to its mastery.

HYPERVENTILATION

There is a physiological sequel called hyperventilation that we simply must call attention to here. Without it there is simply no understanding of what transpires in some of the more advanced uses of the respiratory technique. What happens as one goes on breathing, with longer periods of exhalation, and longer periods of pause, between exhalation and inhalation, is that most of the carbon dioxide within the alveoli of the lungs is blown off, and greater quantities of oxygen are taken in.

(I must insist, for the sake of the readers who have done some reading on the topic of Yoga and meditation, that there is no alternate nostril-breathing recommended here in this essay. There are no gymnastics, occult or physiological, in these simple exercises to train for meditation. I have nothing but respect for Yoga and pranayama. But this process is not being dealt with here. Both nostrils are kept open. The hands are kept relaxed in the lap, and not brought to the face to open or close one or other of the nostrils.)

The result of taking in an excess of oxygen leads to an extraordinary sequence of events that has been noted and recorded by physiologists. Most of them have only observed it as a pathological process. It remained for Wilhelm Reich, the psychiatrist and one-time disciple of Freud, to realize that it could be used as an operational tool in psychotherapy; and modestly, it has been left for me to note that it may be used as a tool for the induction of concentration.

With the inhalation of an excess of oxygen—or with the blowing off of residual carbon dioxide, which is saying the same thing—a chemical change is engineered in the blood-stream, rendering it more alkaline. This, in turn, alters the chemical environment of the brain, so that its essential function is changed. What happens is analogous to stating that the individual becomes drunk, not on alcohol, but on oxygen. The normal flow of thoughts, feelings, and bodily function becomes considerably altered, and the individual, unless he is prepared beforehand by instructions such as this, may be inclined to think he is 'out of the groove'. He *is* actually shaken out of his normal dull kind of functioning, and a wide variety of sensations, physical, emotional, and mental are induced.

The only somatic sequel that he needs to be somewhat on guard against is tetany. This represents tonic spasms, stiffnesses developing in different sets of muscles throughout the body. These differ with each person, because each person has his own peculiar set of muscular tensions that is related to his own individual history and emotional background. *The hyperventilation merely intensifies the muscular tensions already existent, to the point where tetany may occur.*

This phenomenon has been long noted in Yoga literature where it is mentioned that at certain stages of development 'automatic rigidity' may occur, and the body may hop around like a frog. With traditional Yoga breathing or pranayama, this is indeed likely to occur, and it represents a distinct piece of personal progress. With the kind of breathing described in this essay, tetany is almost impossible–save perhaps in a very small minority of shallow-breathers, with a hysterical character-structure, who are also sensitive to surplus of oxygen. The average student to whom this essay is addressed is unlikely to practise for hours at a time, nor to adopt the pranayama technique peculiar to Hatha Yoga practice. So there is nothing to fear on this score. There is no danger here whatsoever.

In the event that a slight hint of tetany does occur, the breathing technique should be momentarily discontinued, and the respiration permitted to resume its normal pattern while one busies oneself with purely routine prosaic tasks. If this is not adequate, then obtain a large brown paper bag, and breath into it. In this manner, one inspires one's own carbon dioxide, quickly rendering the blood more acid, in which case the tetany, due to over-alkalination, will disappear. More often than not, it will ease up by itself without anything being done about it.

The only significant symptoms that we need to mention here are: the development of powerful tinglings all over the body, a delightful feeling of relaxation of muscular tensions, dizziness and lightheadedness, pulsations of energy flowing from head to toe, feelings of considerable pleasure, and sensations of quivering and inner trembling which eventually produce a wonderful sense of ease and release.

Hyperventilation sometimes engineers affective discharge, so that one may feel inclined either to laugh almost hysterically, or to break down and dissolve in tears. Should either of these phenomena occur there is no need for alarm. Merely regard them as distinct stages of progress that result in the discharge of repressed emotions and feelings, and realize that once these feelings have been released, the ability to concentrate is enormously enhance.

KOANS

These, however, are the crucial moments, (just when the function of the brain and central nervous system have undergone radical change), when one should employ every known device to *aspire* eagerly and enthusiastically to the highest. The prayers of old-time or magical invocations or the modern-day affirmations will now prove to be pre-eminently useful. Mantras initiated at this point will be taken up *sua sponte* and act almost as though they were Zen *koans*.

What is a *koan*? According to most authorities, the *koan* is, in effect, not a puzzle to be cleverly solved by an agile monkey-mind; nor is it merely a psychological device to shift or shock the previously fragile ego of a student into a newer species of equilibrium. Certainly it is not a paradox, save to those who have never perceived it from within. It is, however, a simple, clear and direct statement issuing from a specific state of consciousness that it has helped to elicit.

An affirmation or invocation, hence, engaged in at this particular point of development, will exalt the student to the highest state of spiritual consciousness that he is then capable of reaching. Its use may help to precipitate the enlightenment towards which he has been working for so long. It is like placing an arrow in a taut bow. When the cord is released, the arrow is shot with force to its mark. 'I have aimed at the peeled wand of my God, and I have hit; yea, I have hit.'

SUSPENSION OF BREATH

Having spoken of full breathing and hyperventilation, I should make mention, briefly, of another phenomenon which is the diametrical opposite. When some of the higher results of meditation appear, the breathing sometimes appear to become wholly suspended. In reality, it is a very light, fine breathing, existing as it were under the diaphragm–of called interior breathing–which has been nicely described by the ancient Taoists as being 'like the breathing of the infant in the womb.'

FURTHER BREATHING TECHNIQUES

There is an age-old variation of breathing technique which is exquisite in its simplicity, and miraculous in its effect. No rhythm is deliberately set up in the breathing process. No attempt is made to regulate it in any way. One merely breathes in a natural ordinary way. But as one does, one simply notes 'The breath flows in. The breath flows out.' And that is all. It sounds so simple, and basically it is.

In so doing, one may become exquisitely aware of the nostrils, against which the incoming tide of air hits; then, after a while, of the turbinates, the upper portions of the nose; later, of the throat and then of the bronchial tree and the lungs themselves. It might be worth while to imagine the air, incoming and outgoing, as a white mist that one is capable of observing and tracing. And as one does all this, lo! and behold! One is concentrating.

Finally, as a result of these breathing practices and the acquisition of concentration, one may become aware of the fact that one is becoming enormously vitalized. The impression is that of being saturated with cosmic energy that flows through every cell and pore of one's being. At this stage of practice, one needs to learn to circulate the energy–and in this way, to return to a theme of an earlier page–to drain out the energy from the mind. When this kind of skill has been achieved, one merely has to think and lightly will that energy to move and of course it moves. There are several methods of circulation.

CIRCULATION OF ENERGY

The ancient Qabalistic approach is to concentrate on the crown of the head, imagining this to be the centre of one's spiritual life, which is the Universal Self; and, while so doing, to imagine and will that all the energies in the lower areas of the body are gradually being pulled up, sucked up as it were, to the light above the crown of the head. Persistency is required, practice being engaged in day after day. One of these days, while working, so Vitvan says, there is an inner explosion, the electrical circuit is, as it were, completed, and illumination occurs. One *knows*. Not with a knowing of the brain or mind, but with a realization of one's divine ancestry and divine nature–the goal of all mystical work, and the beginning of spiritual freedom.

The full method is rather more detailed, and is described at some length in *Attract and Use Healing Energy, A Small Gem* by Israel Regardie, published by New Falcon Publications. This information can be found in the essay in chapter 3 - *The Art of True Healing*, page 39. It consists basically of the visualization of five centres within the organism and the vibration of certain Qabalistic names within those centres. This develops or releases vast quantities of energy that are circulated in a variety of ways until the organism is enclosed within a vast spinning sphere of light-energy.

A similar method of circulation was once employed by the Chinese Taoist of long ago. The student who is interested should Richard Wilhelm's translation of an ancient Chinese text included in Jung's *Secret of the Golden Flower*.

Once this stage is reached, as a result of upright posture and simple breathing and mantra practice, the achievement of concentration at will has become a fact. From this point on, some of the classical practices can be instituted because through them the attainment of the mystical experience becomes a possibility. Call it Union with God, or the discovery of the Inner Self, or the Realization of the Buddha-nature, this is the goal to be aimed at once concentration is a faculty that has been developed.

VISUALIZATION OF OBJECTS

Perfectly prosaic objects can be taken, visualized and concentrated upon. For example, here is one classical set of instructions for *Dharana*, the control of thought, which could be most useful at this particular stage:

1. Constrain the mind to concentrate itself upon a single simple object imagined.

The five tatvas are useful for this purpose: they are: a black oval; a blue disk; a silver crescent; a yellow square; a red triangle.

2. Proceed to combinations of simple objects; e.g. a black oval within a yellow square, and so on.

3. Proceed to simple moving objects, such as a pendulum swinging, a wheel revolving, etc. Avoid living objects.

4. Proceed to combinations of moving objects, e.g. a piston rising and falling while a pendulum is swinging. The relation between the two movements should be varied in different experiments.

Or even a system of flywheels, eccentrics, and governor.

5. During these practices the mind must be absolutely confined to the object determined upon; no other thought must be allowed to intrude upon the consciousness. The moving systems must be regular and harmonious.

6. Note carefully the duration of the experiments, the number and nature of the intruding thoughts, the tendency of

the object itself to depart from the course laid out for it, and any other phenomena which may present themselves. Avoid overstrain; this is very important.

THE USE OF HYPNOTISM

One more approach needs to be considered. This concerns the cooperation of another trained person. It seems to me that hypnotic suggestion in the hands of a reliable teacher trained in meditation could be enormously valuable. It does not eliminate the need for discipline and prolonged practice. Not by any means. But it may make the achievement of discipline and practice easier for some types of students.

There is no reason why, if the student is found to be suggestible, the meditation teacher should not arrange several hypnotic sessions in which some basic notions are laid down. It could be suggested (once the elementary and preliminary hypnotic induction has been found to be effective) that the student should practice daily. A previous discussion should have determined how often and when the student could practise and whether he wishes to do so. Then the number of practices will be carefully stated during hypnosis, and the length of time to be devoted for each practice period. The teacher could then wait for some considerable time to see whether the student was cooperating, or responding to the hypnotic suggestions.

If there is a reasonable response, then the hypnotic suggestions could be extended. For example, suggestions could be given that henceforth the student will find it easy, at the practice period at such and such a time, morning, noon and/or evening, to concentrate all his mental powers on a series of pre-arrange topics, symbols, or concepts. It may require considerable emphasis and repetition for these suggestions to become effective; but there is no reason on earth why they should not become effective.

The usual argument against this kind of technical approach is that it eliminates the student's personal responsibility; that it is not self-induced and self-devised. This argument is altogether without foundation. The student is still obliged to practice, and practice hard and faithfully. He will have discussed with his teacher what should and should not be suggested in hypnosis, and has given his entire assent to the procedure. But it is still his mind that he has to concentrate, and he will have to devote considerable time and effort to achieve success. Nothing is changed in the traditional procedures, except perhaps that an additional help-incentive or motive has been added.

In this connection, it should always be remembered that all hetero-suggestion becomes, in the last resort, auto-suggestion. It is suggestion given to, and accepted by oneself, but with the aid of a second party.

In one sense, this help has always been recognized. Sometimes the student was permitted to meditate in the company or atmosphere of the teacher. If the student had made a transference to the teacher, or was deeply, devoted to him, such a practice had been known to be of considerable service. Sometimes group meditations have been resorted to. It has been theorized that, if a group of students practise together in a meditation hall–as is common within the confines of Zen Buddhism–all benefit enormously by becoming more concentrated more quickly and more easily.

I do not doubt the efficacy of any of these procedures. It is merely my contention that if these are valid, then hypnotic suggestion is also valid and should be used in certain cases as a means of disposing of stubborn psychological resistances and obstacles.

I should mention that while performing these exercises of every type, a record should be kept. A book or diary should be maintained just for the purpose of entering up the practices performed, the time of the day, the mood one happened to be in, the kind of weather generally prevailing, and any other conditions that you happen to be aware of that may have some bearing on the experiments performed. Make the record of comprehensive, though not necessarily lengthy, as possible. One day in the future, after some attainment has been reached, this will be seen to have considerable value. And if you are lucky enough to have the guidance of a teacher of any degree or grade, he will want to see the record to know how thorough you may or may not have been.

THE FINAL UNION

The instruction quoted above mentioned only the most prosaic of objects to use for constraining the mind to a single point. On the other hand, objects that have a religious or mystical or occult significance more often than not produce results more quickly. And while we are advised to 'work without lust of result', this attitude is the result of, rather than a prerequisite to, the mystical experience. Once one has discovered the God within, the nature of all one's reactions to oneself, one's environment (which is seen to be self-created) and to all else undergoes a massive revolution. One of these changes, of course, is so to function that the fruits of action are of no concern to us. This is Karma Yoga in the true sense of the word. The results are the concern of God, and that is all.

Meditation consists in turning the concentrated mind to any particular topic that requires attention. All the previous discussions were devoted toward developing concentration, without which so-called meditation is merely wool-gathering and uncontrolled fantasy. Meditation based upon concentration eventuates in a union between the meditator and that which is meditated upon, the union of the subject and object, the union of God and Man. Regardless of the language employed to describe it–whether we use Eastern terms such as *Dhyana* and *Samadhi*, or the achievement of *Moksha* or *Mukti*–this is the goal towards which meditation is aimed.

It represents freedom and liberty in the fullest and most philosophical sense of the words. The unity and universality of life, love and beauty are the spiritual components of the enlightenment that is realized with awe, wonder and true spirituality. 'The earth is the Lord's and the fullness thereof'. And since *Tat tvam asi* is seem in meditation to be the truth, the Meditator and the Lord are one.

So to what end, all of this hard work, discipline and constant prayer, this appalling labour to develop concentration? Some of the goals aimed at have been simply described: I doubt if anything is to be gained by a great deal of rhetoric or description of the mystical states sought after or aspired towards. However, to close this essay, I can do no better than to quote, as an example, the illuminations of Jacob Boehme one of the greatest Christian mystics of any age.

Sitting one day in his room, 'his eyes fell upon a burnished pewter dish, which reflected the sunshine with such marvellous splendour that he fell into an inward ecstasy, and it seemed to him as if he could now look into the principles and deepest foundations of things. He believed that it was only a fancy, and in order to banish it from his mind he went out upon the green. But here he remarked that he gazed into the very heart of things, the very herbs and grass, and that actual nature harmonized with what he had inwardly seen. He said nothing of this to anyone, but praised and thanked God in silence.'

Not too long after this initial illumination, 'he was again surrounded by the divine light and replenished with the heavenly knowledge; insomuch as going abroad in the fields to a green before Neys Gate, at Goerlitz, he there sat down and, viewing the herbs and grass of the field in his inward light, he saw their essences, use and properties, which were discovered to him by their lineaments, figures and signatures. In like manner he beheld the whole creation, and from that foundation he afterwards wrote his book, *De Signature Rerum*. In the unfolding of those mysteries before his understanding he had a great measure of joy, yet returned home and took care of his family and lived in great peace and silence, scarcely intimating to any these wonderful things that had befallen him.'

FURTHER READING

Art of Meditation, Joel Goldsmith.
Patanjali's Yoga Aphorisms, William Q. Judge.
Science of Breath, Yogi Ramachraka.
Part One of Book Four, Frater Perdurabo (Aleister Crowley).
Concentration and Meditation, Buddhist Lodge (London).
Meditation, Vitvan (School of the Natural Order).
The Zen Koan, Ruth Fuller Sasaki.
Spiritual Exercises, St. Ignatius of Loyola.
Man's Highest Purpose, Karel Weinfurter.
The Way of the Pilgrim, translated from the Russian by
 R.M. French.

Chapter 2

QABALISTIC PRIMER

*A Layman's Guide to
The Tree of Life*

The Qabalah is an archaic system of Jewish mysticism. S.L. MacGregor Mathers in his learned introduction on this subject wrote many years ago that the principal doctrines of the Qabalah were designed to solve the following problems:

1. The Supreme Being, His nature and attributes.
2. Cosmogony.
3. The creation of angels and man.
4. The destiny of man and angels.
5. The nature of the soul.
6. The nature of angels, demons, and elementals.
7. The import of the revealed law.
8. The transcendental symbolism of numerals.
9. The peculiar mysteries contained in the Hebrew letters.
10. The equilibrium of contraries.

Christian Ginsburg, L.L.D., a hostile critic of some fifty years ago, wished to differentiate between a Jewish mysticism on the one hand and the Qabalah on the other. His unsympathetic attitude was predicated on the narrowness of so-called nineteenth-century rationalism. This attitude has since been discarded in the sciences as it has been in the study of mysticism.

That Ginsburg's intransigent point of view is no longer valid is strongly stressed by one of the most inclusive of all modern Hebraic scholars, Gershom G. Scholem. In his masterful work, *The Kaballah and its Symbolism*, he states simply that the Qabalah literally means 'tradition'. As such, it is the tradition of divine things, an esoteric tradition. Thus, it is the sum of Jewish mysticism.

He proceeds further by adding that it has had a long history, far longer and more stable than has hitherto been suspected. For centuries it has exerted a profound religious and philosophical influence on those of the Jewish people who were desirous of deepening their understanding of the more prosaic or orthodox forms and conceptions of Judaism. For him and many other scholars like him, therefore, Ginsburg's criticism is entirely without meaning, not being rooted in historical fact.

COMMENTARIES AND TRANSLATIONS

The Qabalah is not a particular book, as some laymen have erroneously assumed. It is a literature–a vast literature, much of it belonging to the Middle Ages and some to earlier Gnostic periods. Most of it still remains in Hebrew and Aramaic. During the mystical renaissance in the eighteenth century in Poland and central Europe, the Chassidic period, the literature underwent expansion, reinterpretation and republication. Some little of this had been translated in German. Rather less of it had appeared in English. A great deal still requires to be rendered into English in order to round out our wholly inadequate knowledge.

Only a few of its major classics are currently available. For example, the *Zohar*, which was translated by Sperling and Simon, was originally published in the 1930s by the Soncino Press in England. The much smaller *Sepher Yetzirah* has long been obtainable in several different translations. Its miniscule size made it a less formidable task of translation than did the *Zohar*.

Some few commentaries and books about different aspects of this literature have been translated or written in English. A great part of this latter material, interestingly enough, has been done by non-Jews who are mystics and occult students. Having found the Qabalah useful and interesting, they did not, however, try to use it as a technical device to convert the people of Israel wholesale to Christ–as has been attempted before. A good part of this more recent work, listed as the end of this essay, has been on a very high level, both from a literary and a didactic point of view, and is likely to survive for quite a long time.

As a Jewish mysticism, the Qabalah is naturally very Jewish. Some books of the Qabalah not only elaborate theories and sectarian explanations based on early Rabbinical exegesis of Old Testament texts and Hebrew belief and history, but differ from most other systems of mysticism by extensive elaboration of the 'chosen people' theme, elevating it into a sort of cosmically determined fact.

This approach may not necessarily be very appealing to many of us today, Christian or Jew. We feel little need for the formal context and content of institutionalized religion of any sect or denomination.

THE TREE OF LIFE

The fundamental basis of the Qabalah from the modern point of view rests not on its mystical speculations about creation, eschatology, the Messiah, the Sabbath, and so on–but on 'The Tree of Life'. This is a simple theoretical and mathematical structure based on a 'filing cabinet' idea.

This essentially illuminating possibility was really laid down in The *Sepher Yetzirah*. Here certain ideas are systematically attributed to the basic system of numbers from one to ten. Furthermore, each of the twenty-two letters of the Hebrew alphabet are elaborated in much the same way–an idea quite intelligible when it is remembered that the Hebrew letters are, at the same time, numbers. The sum total of the ten numerals and the twenty-two letters comprise the thirty-two Paths of Wisdom, as they are called, and represent 'The Tree of Life'.

To each one of these Paths, this early *Book of Formation* attributes planets, zodiacal signs, divine names, elements, directions in space, etc. This is done in such a manner as to formulate rudiments of a filing system. Later generations of scholars and students, by using this root system, have added a complex series of additional data. This includes information from Greek and Egyptian mythology, meditative material derived from the Tarot, information based on mystical experience (visionary and ecstatic), a conglomerate of sounds and smells and colours–perfumes, jewels and, significantly too, modern scientific data. It has become a meaningful syncretism.

THE ORGANIZATION OF KNOWLEDGE

The whole *mélange* thus serves as a further means of classifying all knowledge. It serves to organize the contents of the mind and to provide a mechanism for unifying all systems of any and every kind of knowledge to unity. And so we return to the heart, not simply of the Jewish Qabalah, but of all mysticism: 'For I have found Thee alike in the Me and the Thee; there is no difference, O my beautiful, my desirable One! In the One and the Many have I found Thee: yea, I have found Thee.'

Once the potentiality of this root idea is grasped, it can be seen as infinitely more important, significant and useful than any quasi-mystical theory of cosmogenesis or anthropogenesis. It is far more productive and vastly more creative than esoteric hypothesis as to why the Jews were selected as the chosen people, what went on in heaven during the Exile, or how the Messiah weeps on high on learning of the privations and sorrows of the dispersed people of Israel. Any archaic psychology or Christology or theology fades into minor importance when it is placed on the Tree and perceived in relation to other data from similar esoteric systems.

The subject of the Qabalah is so vast that in order to manage it more intelligently an arbitrary division of its content material should be made into four specific segments. We must remember at all times, however, that the division is wholly arbitrary and for our convenience only. Each section is really without any dividing line, spilling over and spreading into every other section.

1. *Comparative.* By using the Tree of Life as a mathematical structure, a science of comparative religion and mysticism is brought within the bounds of possibility. It can be employed to heighten understanding by relating one set of known concepts to others in a far different and distant system, thus reducing the many to the One. This essay is concerned solely with an elementary introduction to this theme.

2. *Doctrinal.* This consists of a mystico-theological exposition of some of the great problems that have always preoccupied mankind. The traditional Qabalah has its own unique points of view. I doubt, however, that it has too much validity in today's world. Nevertheless, it is a distinct attitude, and as such is to be respected and compared to other esoteric systems.

3. *Theurgic.* This has also been called the magical or wonder-working tradition of the Qabalah. It is strongly rooted in the esoteric traditions relating to The Tree of Life, which has its roots in the divine, secret life of God. In effect, the entire theory and practice revolve around the 'way of return' to the Godhead from which man has become alienated. The more modern interpretations of technical procedures and methodology are vastly different from and superior to the more ancient and specifically Jewish point of view. It is in effect a more universal, eclectic approach rooted in that curious phenomenon of the last century, the genius of the Hermetic Order of the Golden Dawn.

4. *Exegetical.* Some contemporaries who know no Hebrew, and who have received no schooling or discipline in these aspects of the Qabalah, have written foolishly that these methods are unimportant. This is to be understood as merely

a frank confession of their own lack of experience and understanding. The tryo (a beginner or novice) who has developed even minor facility in the use of these techniques or exegesis opens himself to fantastic insights, which, in their own way, are relevant mystical experiences.

It is this latter, the realization of the universe as being divine, the entire body of God which includes every man and every form of life within its vastness, which is the goal of *all* mysticism. If this technical approach can yield this ultimate goal, its employment is not to be sneered at or minimized.

THE TEN SEPHIROTH

The outstanding feature of The Tree of Life once we begin to examine it closely, is revealed as a system of the ten *Sephiroth* or divine emanations, divided into three columns. There is a right and a left column of three *Sephiroth* each, and a middle one of four. The right one is called the Pillar of Mercy; the left, the Pillar of Severity–the prototypes of the Masonic pillars of *Yachin* and *Boaz*. One of these is male, the other female; one is positive, the other negative. One is white, the other is black. And so on–the eternal play of the opposites: 'Remember that unbalanced force is evil, that unbalanced severity is but cruelty and oppression, but that also unbalanced mercy is but weakness which would allow and abet evil.'

Thus the Qabalah stresses a middle way between the two opposites, indicating the age-old need for the avoidance of extremes. This attitude is also found in Hindu philosophy, in Buddhism, and in modern terms is one of the major goals of Jungian psychology.

The extremes are one-sided spiritual and psychological attitudes which can only lead to total disintegration of the human spirit. They point to the need for the union of the two opposites in a new and higher integrity.

The Middle Pillar thus becomes symbolic of the 'way of return', the path of redemption, as it were. A vast system both of esoteric theory and magical practice has been erected on these structures.

THE FOUR WORLDS

Another way of looking at the Tree is by way of the Four Worlds. These levels are known as *Atziluth*, or the Archetypal World; *Briah*, the Creative World; *Yetzirah*, The Formative World, and *Assiah*, the World of Action, the Material World. These in turn are attributed to the four letters of the divine name, often referred to as the Tetragrammaton, which simply means the four-lettered name of YHVH. Now this refers not simply to the Jehovah of the Old Testament, who appears to have been a provincial, racial and testy old tutelary deity, but to the basic creative force in action of the *Ain Soph*, the Infinite. The old name is retained but is given an entirely new and broad interpretation.

Y is *Yod*, attributed to the element of fire, and is called the Father; it is the archetype of all things, and the area, as it were, of God and His divine names. H, *Heh*, the first H of Tetragrammaton, is the Mother, referred to the element of water, the creative world where the archangelic forces hold sway and function, carrying out the creative impulses received from on high. V is *Vau*, the Son, referred to the element of air, and to the Formative World, where the angelic forces fashion and form the prototypes of all things on the imaginative basis previously laid down. The final H, *Heh*, is referred to the Daughter, the element of earth, where all the intrinsic factors of the higher creative forces become embodied.

All is God and His creative energy, from the highest to the lowest–for there is nothing that is not God. It is only the limitations of our sensory structure that prevent us from perceiving that we live and move and have our being in the Godhead, here and now.

Westcott affirms that 'Man is still the copy of God on earth; his form is related to the Tetragrammaton of Jehovah, YHVH, for in a diagram *Yod* is as the head, *Heh* the arms, *Vau* the body, and the final H, *Heh*, the lower limbs.'

THE PENTAGRAMMATON

One of the letters of the Hebrew alphabet is *Shin*. In the *Book of Formation* it is given the attribution of fire, and, by another mathematical process, it becomes the symbol of the Holy Spirit. Tradition sponsors the insertion of this letter into the middle of the four-lettered Name, splitting it asunder, thus forming YHshVH, the Pentagrammaton or five-lettered Name. This combination of letters represents the illumination of the elemental or natural man by the descent and impact of the Holy Spirit. As thus formed, the name represents the God-man, symbolized in Christianity by Christ descending on the man Jesus. Jesus, by this symbolism, represents the natural man who, by devotion and meditation and the theuric process, opened his human nature to the brilliant descent of the Light.

It is this enlightenment that all men are destined to enjoy at some far-distant time in human evolution. It is this that separates man *qua* man from the God-man, the goal of all mysticism. All mystical techniques, including those of the Qabalah, represent a method of hastening the slow tedious process of human evolution so that the states of consciousness that we are told will ultimately occur routinely in mankind may dawn today.

The ten digits or files of The Tree of Life are the manifold expression of deity conceived of as the creative power of the Primal Light. This is labelled as *Ain Soph*–the infinite, serving as the absolute, unknown and unknowable diving ground of Being. It is from this Nothingness that creation takes place, creation in and from Its essence, descending and ascending in various degrees of clarity or obscurity (to us only), resulting in the appearance of several emanations that are labeled *Sephiroth*.

Incidentally, this word *Sephiroth* is a feminine plural form of the word *Sephirah*. In *The Book of Formation* the word *Sephiroth* is variously translated as numbers, letters and sounds. Creation is conceived to be a divine magical act symbolized by the employment of the letters of the Hebrew alphabet. These letters are not merely symbols of magical forces; they *are* the creative forces of the universe. This assumed fact underlies all magical ritual and theurgic process. As one of the Golden Dawn rituals put it: 'By names and images are all powers awakened and re-awakened.' Ritual action not only represents symbolically the divine life; it evokes the interior spiritual force manifested in concrete symbols.

I must emphasize here the fact that this is only an elementary and suggestive treatise. There is no attempt made to follow an orderly pattern of exposition. It is essentially a kind of free association that I am pursuing. When the student can follow this simple rambling exposition without too much difficulty, then he can turn with confidence to some of the more systematic and complex delineations of the system.

KETHER

The first *Sephirah* is known as *Kether*, the Crown, and represents a concentration of light-energy within the infinity of *Ain Soph*. The Qabalistic theory has it that from the Infinite, the creative impulse proceeded in a flash of radiant light (*Zohar*). This released the creative powers of the Infinite, resulting in a point or focus of multifaceted potentiality and development. In addition to the Crown, it is also known as the Smooth Point, Macroprosopus or the Great Face and a host of other symbolic images and names, and is the first or opening *Sephirah* on the Tree.

In other mythologies it is represented by Amoun 'The Concealed One' and the 'Opener of the Day', as well as by Ptah the divine potter who forms all things on his revolving wheel. One of the several attributions of *Kether* is *Raysheeth ha-gilgoleem*, the first wheelings or whirlings–as though to imply the earliest spiral nebula movements. All beginnings, all seeds, of all things represented by One, find their place in this part of the filing cabinet. One of the really great, though less well-known, American occult teachers defines it as 'The Power to be Conscious', a very eloquent phrase.

Another of its many associations is Metatron, the Angel of the Presence who, avers the ancient mythology, was changed into a fiery flame. We know from the Bible that God is a burning fire. Yet another attribution is the choir of angels known as the *Chayoth ha-Qadesh*, Beings seen by Ezekiel in his vision. The opening of the Book of Ezekiel is work re-reading at this juncture.

This prophet's vision of the Lord riding upon the fiery chariot of the Holy Living Creatures, accompanied by supernal visions and voices, movements and upheavals on earth–all of this well outside the range of the spiritual experiences of most other Biblical personalities–was for the Qabalist a real opening into higher realms. It represented an unveiling of the innermost and impenetrable secrets locked up in the newly-revealed interrelation of man and God. It was ever interpreted as a sort of divine self-unveiling, an ineffable mystical experience of the highest magnitude. The Qabalists considered that the door to the beyond was flung wide open so that the properly prepared individual, at the direct invitation of God, could mount as though on a flaming Pegasus and chariot to the secret spiritual lief that he has laboured for so long to reach.

The chariot (the *Merkabah*) was thus a 'mystic way' leading to the veritable heights of the Tree of Life, to the Crown of all. It was considered a vehicle by means of which the Qabalist was carried directly to face-to-face encounter with his highest divinity. It was the aim of the would-be mystic, therefore, to be a '*Merkabah*-rider' so that he might be enabled while still incarnate as a human being to ascend to his spiritual El Dorado. Enlightenment is thus the meaning of all the 'chariot' symbolisms.

CHOKMAH

Chokmah, or Wisdom, is the name of the second emanation or manifestation. It is alluded to above all other representations of the primal duality as fatherhood, maleness, wisdom, the positive pole–all these associations are represented here. There are archangels and angels attributed to each one of these *Sephiroth*, representing the emergence of different forms or types of the divine creative power and intent.

The divine name used in the Old Testament is said to be *Yah*. The archangel is Ratziel, the Mystery of God, while its astrological attribution refers to the wheel of the zodiac itself, as though to indicate its supraterrestrial sphere of influence.

In the prologue of the *Zohar*, the Book of Splendour, it is a beautiful myth expatiating on the biblical verse 'In the beginning God created...'. By way of preamble, it is necessary to indicate that the Hebrew words for this are '*be-Raysheeth bara Elohim*...'. A literal translation is as follows:

B' means 'In'

Raysheeth–'the beginning'

Bara–'created'

Elohim–translated as God. (But the word *El* is God. *Eloh* would be a feminine God, the suffix oh determining the feminine gender. The other suffix *im* is a masculine form of plurality. In the word *Sephiroth*, for example, the suffix *oth* represents the feminine form of plurality.)

The first letter of the Bible therefore is b, *Beth*, as it is also of the second word *bara*, to create.

The Zoharic myth I refer to deals with the Hebrew letters as beings or personifications of the creative forces which one by one parade before God asking for the privilege of being the first to describe the process of creation: 'When the Holy One, blessed be he, was about to make the world, all the letters of the alphabet were still embryonic... When He came to create the world, all the letters advanced themselves before Him in reversed order.'

One by one, they describe why they and they alone should be so chosen, and one by one, arguments are tendered to deny them this privilege. Finally the letter B (in Hebrew *Beth*) entered the scene, and said:

'"O Lord of the world, may it please Thee to put me first in the creation of the world, since I represent the benedictions (*berakhoth*) offered to Thee on high and below." The Holy One, blessed be he, said to her: "Assuredly, with thee I will create the world, and thou shalt form the beginning in the creation of the world."'

The entire emphasis on this play on words and letters is really to elicit the concept, so necessary for man, of the benevolence and benediction of the Creative Power. It would have been very difficult for early man to have lived without this belief.

And thus it came to be that the letter *Beth* opens up the biblical account of creation. Now, using the comparative method made possible by our filing cabinet, we find that to B, the number 2, in the *Sepher Yetzirah,* the planet Mercury is attributed, and so its god is Hermes who is a lower form of the Egyptian Thoth, the god of 'wisdom and utterance, the god that cometh forth from the veil.' Thoth is said to have pronounced the magickal words that formed the whole gamut of created things. In the particular exordium of the Golden Dawn, there is the following significant passage:

At the ending of the Night; at the limits of the Light, Thoth stood before the Unborn Ones of Time!

Then was formulated the Universe;

Then came forth the Gods thereof;

The Aeons of the Bornless Beyond:

Then was the Voice vibrated:

Then was the Name declared.

At the Threshold of the Entrance, between the Universe and the Infinite,

In the Sign of the Enterer, stood Thoth as before him were the Aeons proclaimed.

In Breath did he vibrate them; in Symbols did he record them.

For betwixt The Light and the Darkness did he stand.

This entire passage from the Golden Dawn teaching is worthy of prolonged meditation. It should be related in meditation to the following idea from Dion Fortune's book on the Qabalah:

In order to contact *Chokmah* we must experience the rush of the dynamic cosmic energy in its pure form; an energy so tremendous that mortal man is fused into disruption by it. It is recorded that when Semele, mother of Dionysos, saw Zeus her divine lover in his god-form as the Thunderer, she was blasted and burnt, and gave birth to her divine son prematurely. The spiritual experience assigned to *Kether* is the Vision of God face to face; and God (Jehovah) said to Moses, 'Thou canst not look upon my face and live.'

But although the sight of the Divine Father blasts mortals as with fire, the Divine Don comes familiarly among them and can be invoked by the appropriate rites–Bacchanalia in the case of the Son of Zeus, and the Eucharist in the case of the Son of Jehovah. Thus we see that there is a lower form of manifestation, which 'shews us the Father', but that this rite owes its validity solely to the fact that it derives its Illuminating Intelligence, its Inner Robe of Glory, from the Father, *Chokmah*.

BINAH

Binah, Understanding, is the third *Sephirah*, and is feminine and negative in polarity. To *Binah* is attributed amongst other things the *Shekinah*, a symbol of the Holy Spirit. This is a fascinating set of concepts since it emerged in Judaic thought, which in its monotheism is male-oriented without a diluting trace of any feminine influence. The one exception possibly is in the constant devotional reference to the Sabbath as a Bride–and on this concept a vast mystical superstructure has been erected. It connects the Sabbath with the *Shekinah*, and while apparently using biblical texts as authority, some Qabalistic books force the emergence of a symbolism or a mythos which is in every way feminine and thus unalterable opposed to the historical development of non-mystical Judaism. It is reminiscent of Jung's idea of enantiodromia, that any psychological trend sooner or later must evoke or pass into its opposite–the Taoist idea that each element of *Yang* or *Yin* contains the seed or root of its own opposite. 'At the height of the *Yang* (the male) the *Yin* (female) is born.'

In orthodox Judaic literature, the *Shekinah*–a word meaning literally the indwelling presence of God–is taken to mean simply God himself in His Omnipresent activity in the world, and of course in Israel. His presence, what the Bible calls His 'face', is in Rabbinical usage His indwelling presence in the world. Nowhere in the conventional orthodox literature is a distinction made between God Himself and His *Shekinah*. The *Shekinah* is not there as a special hypostasis distinguished from God as a whole. God is transcendent; His *Shekinah* is immanent.

So far as concerns the Qabalah, however, the *Shekinah* is conceived as an aspect of God, a quasi-independent feminine element within Him. She is also conceived as the dwelling place of the human soul, an entirely new conception. The idea that man's highest self had its origin in the feminine precinct within God Himself is an outstanding and far-reaching contribution of the Qabalah to mystical thought. It bears many similarities to Eastern philosophy, especially to the Vedanta.

It as once differentiates the Qabalah from the hitherto masculine sterility of orthodox Judaic belief, so top-heavy without a feminine component, and permits a well-defined comparison, within the format of The Tree of Life, with such feminine potencies in other esoteric systems such as the Holy Ghost, Kwan Yin, Shakti, Mother Durga, Aditi the Light-mother, and Mary the mother of Jesus. They may not be wholly identical, but there remains nonetheless enormous similarities which render the possibility of concretizing a true science of comparative mystical religion.

All of this aids in our understanding of *Binah* as the great Mother, the wide open sea which has given birth to us all, the planet Saturn, sombre and grave, and old Chronos, the father of Time. Crowley has likened her to our Lady Babalon, the mother of all whoredoms–and while the language is at first startling to a degree, it accords entirely with the Eastern concept of Kali, the giver of life and death, the lover of every man, capable of infinite conceptions. Ramakrishna's devotion to Kali, to the divine Mother, is an outstanding example of this.

These three *Sephiroth* are often spoken of as the Supernals–far removed from and transcending the operations and functions of the other areas of The Tree of Life. Seen as a unity, these three are referred to simply as *Aimah Elohim*, the Mother of the Gods, to whom are given the three Vedantic characteristics of *Sat-Chit-Ananda*–Being, Wisdom and Ecstasy. Played against these are their Buddhist opposites of *Anatta, Anicca*, and *Dukkham*–Unsubstantiality, Impermanence and Sorrow. The opposites are, paradoxically, identical in this transcendent area of the Tree.

Separating the divine transcendence from the more familiar and more readily conceivable aspects of the Tree, there is said to stretch a vast gulf, an abyss between noumenon and phenomenon, which is wholly unbridgeable by man. So long as he remains man, bound up in his private world of reason and practical events, the Supernals are abstract unreachable concepts. Only by riding the *mercabah* or the mystical experience, resulting in the destruction of *ahamkara*, the ego-making faculty, can the abyss be traversed. The tradition here is so vast, so complex, and so abstract that we have to be content at this moment with just this reference, and no more.

The planetary attribution is Saturn, stability and form, form which binds energy, as *purusha* is embodied in *prakriti* according to the Sankhya system of Kapila. Its archangel is merely the Hebrew name for Saturn, *Shabbathai*, with the 'el' appended as a suffix–at least so it is according to the *Sigillum Dei Aemeth* of the Dee-Kelly system, making Shabbathiel, or Tzaphkiel in the more traditional system. The divine name is *YHVH Elohim*, a compound of Tetragrammaton plus the masculine plural of a female god.

The *Sephirah* is ambivalent, or rather, as a true symbol, bipolar. In the lovely Crowleyan symbolism, *Binah* is the City of the Pyramids under the Night of Pan, where the adept who has crossed the abyss as a successful *mercabah*-rider, and so annihilated the ego, becomes a Babe of the Abyss nursed by our Lady Babalon.

As a final comment relative to *Binah*, there is a short paragraph by Dion Fortune which is pertinent hereto:

> The expansive force given off by petrol is pure energy, but it will not drive a car. The constrictive organization of *Binah* is potentially capable of driving a car, but it cannot do so unless set in motion by the expansion of the stored-up energy of petrol-vapour. *Binah* is all-potential, but inert. *Chokmah* is pure energy, limitless and tireless, but incapable of doing anything except radiate off into space if left to its own devices. But when *Chokmah* acts upon *Binah*, its energy is gathered up and set to work. When *Binah* receives the impulse of *Chokmah*, all her latent capacities are energized. Briefly, *Chokmah* supplies the energy, and *Binah* supplies the machine.

CHESED

Chesed is the next *Sephirah*. The Hebrew word means 'mercy'. All significances attached to the number 4 find their place in this filing jacket.

Jupiter is the astrological attribution, from which we obtain ideas of the authority, form, law, abundance, generosity, and order in the Eastern sense of *dharma*–the rightness of things, the proper way. Here too is to be found the Egyptian *Maat*, who wields the feather of Truth.

Its magical symbol or image is that of a crowned and powerful king enthroned on a dais, clothed with the fulsome purples and royal blues associated with his regal status. Around him are the cognate symbols of Jupiterian authority, the orb and the crook. On some of the Egyptian god forms, the crook is pointed to the left shoulder to which *Chesed* is attributed, whilst the flail or the scourge points to the right shoulder, to *Geburah*. The crook or crozier is the shepherd tool of mercy, the pastoral staff of giving aid on the spiritual level.

In this same connection, Zeus is an attribute–the god whose authority and power and energy is so vast that he commands the lightning and the storms, and hurls thunderbolts.

Thus *Chesed* is authority and divine leadership, which produces order out of chaos, permitting freedom and liberty within certain well-defined limits. 'Liberty', wrote Dion Fortune with great sagacity, 'might be defined as the right to choose one's master, for a ruler one must have in all organized corporate life, else there is chaos. It is effectual and inspiring leadership that is the crying need of the world at the present time, and country after country is seeking and finding the ruler who approximates most closely to its national ideal, and is falling in as one man behind him. It is the benign, organizing, ordering Jupiter influence that is the only medicine for the world's sickness; as this comes to bear, the nations will recover their emotional poise and physical health.'

The geometrical form proper to this sphere is the square–reminiscent of the Masonic moral idea of being on the level, on the square; this too is *dharma*. Its Jungian archetypal symbol would probably be the 'wise old man'. Its element is water, reflected downward from *Binah*. Each *Sephirah*, it must be noted, is a fascinating combination of balance of male and female, positive and negative symbols, in equilibrium.

Other titles for *Chesed* are *Gedulah*, greatness or majesty, and *Rachamon*, Mercy. The divine name is *El*, meaning simply God–masculine in nature and grammar. Its archangelic force is called Tzadkiel, the righteousness of God. Its angels are the *Chashmalim,* the Brilliant Ones.

It is the ancient occult view that man is a microcosm of the macrocosm, a replica in miniature of the great world in which he lives, and of which he is a part. Whatever set of forces operate in the vast expanses of the universe about him, these are also represented within man himself. Thus the Tree is not only a symbolic map of the universe; its *Sephiroth* are symbolic representatives of the psychic structure of man as well.

In fact, relative to this, there is a pertinent quotation from the *Zohar*:

> What, then, is man? Does he consist solely of skin, flesh, bones and sinews? Nay, the essence of man is his soul; the skin, flesh, bones and sinews are but an outward covering,

the mere garments, but they are not the man. When man departs (from this world) he divests himself of all these garments. The skin with which he covers himself, and all these bones and sinews, all have a symbolism in the mystery of the Supernal Wisdom, corresponding to that which is above...

The bones and the sinews symbolize the Chariots and the celestial Hosts, which are inward. All these are garments upon that which he covers himself, and all these bones and sinews, all have a symbolism in the mystery of the Supernal Wisdom, corresponding to that which is above... Esoterically, the man below corresponds entirely to the Man above.

GEBURAH

Geburah, Severity, is the fifth *Sephirah.* It counterbalances *Chesed* on the Tree, and in terms of Qabalistic theory is the opposite. Whereas the fourth *Sephirah* represents mercy and kindness and form-building through love and attraction, *Geburah* represents power and energy and, inversely, destruction and tearing down. Both are cosmic processes as well as endopsychic events, neither to be denied or underestimated. If there were only building-up and construction, the universe would soon become a rather cluttered place–the vision of our already over-crowded cities on a cosmic scale. The power involved here ensures that outmoded forms of life and ways of communication, whatever they may be, are broken down and the material re-employment in other and more suitable ways.

It is nicely expressed in Dion Fortune's book in these well-chosen words:

Dynamic energy is as necessary to the welfare of society as meekness, charity, and patience. We must never forget that the eliminatory diet, which will restore health in disease, will produce disease in health. We must never exact the qualities which are necessary to compensate an overplus of force into ends in themselves and the means of salvation. Too much charity is the handiwork of a fool; too much patience is the hallmark of a coward. What we need is a just and wise balance which makes for health, happiness, and sanity all round, and the frank realization that sacrifices are necessary to obtain it. You cannot eat your cake and have it in the spiritual sphere any better than anywhere else.

The divine name is appropriately *Elohim Gibor*, a Powerful God, or the Gods (male and female) of Might. Its planet is Mars, the god of War, expressing the character of Ra Hoor Khuit in *The Book of the Law*: 'Now let it be first understood that I am a god of War and of Vengeance. I shall deal hardly with them…Worship me with fire & blood; worship me with swords & with spears. Let the woman be girt with a sword before me: let blood flow to my name.'

In the book of Exodus, there is a paean of martial joy to Jehovah after the crossing of the Red Sea which had opened up for the children of Israel to pass through, and then closed over the Egyptians with their chariots, destroying them wholly. There He is called *Eesh milchomah*, a Man of War. 'Jehovah is a mighty warrior; Jehovah is His Name!' I can still vividly remember from early boyhood attending the synagogue when this particular portion of the *Torah* was being sung. The entire melody and style of ritual chanting changed triumphantly as the cantor entoned: 'I will sing unto Jehovah, for he hath triumphed gloriously!... Thy right hand, O Jehovah, is become glorious in power; thy right hand O Lord hath dashed the enemy to pieces!... Who is like unto Thee among the Gods, O Jehovah!' (The Hebrew initials of this last sentence were used centuries later to form the neologism 'Macabee'.) No one listening could fail to have the blood freeze in his veins, and the hackles arise on the back of his neck.

Geburah, in a word, is the energy aspect of creativity. All the symbols, from any source, mythological or otherwise, relate exclusively to this notion. Since it is the fifth file in our filing system, all five pointed figures, symbols, ideas, and so forth, are referred here.

Aleister Crowley once wrote a charming little pornographic story called *The Daughter of the Horseleech* which in itself is of no consequence to us here, save for the one redeeming feature of a beautiful description of the entire spiritual hierarchy of *Geburah*, from the divine Name down to the lowliest spirit. It is so well done that it is worth-while quoting the several paragraphs as descriptive of the hierarchical elements:

> The crown of *Elohim Gibor* was Space itself; the two halves of brain were the Yea and Nay of the Universe; his breath was the breath of very Life; his being was the Mahalingam of the First, beyond Life and Death the generator from Nothingness. His armour was the Primal Water of Chaos. The infinite moonlike curve of his body; the flashing swiftness of his Word, that was the Word that formulated that which was beyond Chaos and Cosmos; the might of him,

greater than that of the Elephant and of the Lion and of the Tortoise and of the Bull fabled in Indian legend as the supports of the four letters of the Name; the glory of him, that was even as that of the Sun which is before all and beyond all Suns, of which the stars are little sparks struck off as he battled in the Infinite against the Infinite...

Behold the mighty one, behold *Kamael* the strong! His crownless head was like a whirling wheel of amethyst, and all the forces of the earth and heaven revolved therein. His body was the Mighty Sea itself, and it bore the scars of crucifixion that had made it two score times stronger than it was before. He too bore the wings and weapons of Space and Justice; and in himself he was that great Amen that is the beginning and end of all.

Behind him were the *Seraphim*, the fiery Serpents. On their heads the triple tongues of fire; their glory like unto the Sun, their scales like burning plates of steel; they danced like virgins before their lord, and upon the storm and roar of the sea did they ride in their glory...

All glorious was the moon-like crown of the great Intelligence *Graphiel*. His face was like the Sun as it appears beyond the veil of this earthly firmament. His warrior body was like a tower of steel, virginal strong.

Scarlet were his kingly robes, and his limbs were swathed in young leaves of lotus; for those limbs were stronger than any armour ever forged in heaven or hell. Winged was he with the wings of gold that are the Wind itself; his sword of green fire flamed in his right hand, and in his left he held the blue feather of Justice, unstirred by the wing of his flight, or the upheaval of the universe.

Bartzabel...Of flaming, radiant, far-darting gold was his crown; flashing hither and thither more swiftly than the lightning were its rays. His head was like the Sun in its strength, even at high noon. His cloak was of pure amethyst, flowing behind him like a mighty river; his armour was of living gold, burnished with lightning even to the greaves and the armed feet of him; he radiated an intolerable splendour of gold and he bore the Sword and balance of Justice. Mighty and golden were his wide-flashing wings!

TIPHARETH

Tiphareth (pronounced T'phay-reth) means Beauty, harmony and infers Equilibrium and balance. On The Tree of Life it is the central *Sephirah*, and in many ways is one of the most important sections of our filing cabinet. It is equidistant, as it were, to *Kether* as it is from *Malkuth*, and it has connecting links with practically every other part of the Tree.

The magical images which give meaning to the file are manifold. They include the resurrection gods of every age and clime from Osiris to Christ, the solar discs from Ra to Apollo, gods of spiritual inebriation such as Bacchus and Dionysos, and the newly born spiritual child from Krishna to baby Jesus. Meditation on all these images will reveal the essential nature of the *Sephirah*.

As usual, Dion Fortune expresses herself extremely well in this connection:

The ancients...differentiated between the mantic methods which induced the chthonic, or underworld contacts, and the divine inebriation of the Mysteries. The Maenads rushing in the train of Dionysos were of an entirely different order of initiation to the pythonesses; the pythonesses were psychics and mediums, but he Maenads, the initiates of the Dionysiac Mysteries, enjoyed exaltation of consciousness and a quickening of life that enabled them to perform amazing prodigies of strength.

All the dynamic religions have this Dionysiac aspect; even in the Christian religion many saints have left records of the Crucified Christ of their devotion coming to them at last as the Divine Bridegroom; and when they speak of this divine inebriation that comes to them, their language uses the metaphors of human love as its appropriate express–"How lovely art thou, my sister, my spouse'; 'Faint from the kisses of the lips of God...' These things tell a great deal to those who have understanding.

Its more immediate astrological symbol is the sun with its almost infinite number of attributions and significances, which should be studied and meditated upon to get the full impact of the *Sephirah*.

Its divine name is *YHVH Eloah ve-Daath*, rather difficult or meaningless to translate literally, but may be rendered as YHVH, Lord God of Knowledge. The archangel is Raphael, the healing of God, which might remind us of Exodus, 15:26: 'For I am the Lord that healeth thee.' *Malachim* is a Hebrew word meaning angels; if the second 'a' is omitted, it may be translated as 'kings'.

Perhaps one of the best ways of elucidating the full meaning of this *Sephirah* is to quote one of the Golden Dawn ritual speeches from a document known as Z-1:

> For Osiris on-Nophris who is found perfect before the Gods, hath said:
>
> These are the Elements of my Body.
>
> Perfected through suffering, glorified through trail.
>
> For the scent of the dying rose is as the repressed sign of my suffering:
>
> And the flame-red fire as the energy of mine undaunted will;
>
> And the cup of Wine is the pouring out of the blood of my Heart.
>
> Sacrificed unto regeneration, unto the new Life.
>
> And the bread and salt are as the foundations of my body
>
> Which I destroy in order that they may be renewed.
>
> For I am Osiris triumphant, even Osiris on-Nophiris the Justified.
>
> I am He who is clothed with the body of flesh,
>
> Yet in whom is the Spirit of the great Gods.
>
> I am the Lord of Life, triumphant over death.
>
> He who partaketh with me shall arise with me;
>
> I am the manifestor in matter of Those whose abode is the Invisible.
>
> I am purified; I stand upon the universe.
>
> I am its reconciler with the eternal Gods.
>
> I am the Perfector of Matter.
>
> And without me, the Universe is not.

NETZACH

Netzach, Victory, is the seventh section of our filing cabinet. By using the English translation, we can consider *Nike*, with a firm stride forward, with wings apart and ablaze with fire and fury, as the symbolic image for our meanings.

The divine name *YHVH Tzabaoth*, Lord God of Hosts, is equally confirmatory of this theme. We are not dealing with creative imagination here, or with any mental faculty in the ordinary sense of the term, but with the fire of emotion and feeling, which basically are the forces that evoke creativity. These are not merely constituents of the human psyche; they are integral components of the universe itself. The experience of ecstasy, joy, delight and fervour–this is Victory.

Its fire is reflected from *Geburah*, making a well-defined relationship between the astrological polarities of Mars and Venus.

The pantheons filed here are those relating to the astrological attribution of Venus itself. Aphrodite, Astarte, Hathor, and so forth. They represent love, fulfillment, pleasure, the arts in all their forms, and beauty.

Just as in a horoscope, the seventh house represents marriage, but the fifth house represents pleasure, creativity, and sex, so *Netzach* may include love, pleasure and sexuality (or polarity), but it is *Yesod* which refers to productivity and fertility. There is no necessary relationship between one and the other; each may co-exist by itself.

Netzach refers to the emotions and feelings which may bring about a union of the two poles, but it is *Yesod* and the moon and its inner psychic tides that permit this coupling to result in offspring.

Netzach may be said to refer to the desire-nature, to what the East calls *Kama*, desire, wish, need, lust.

The approach to God, as a technical mystical way of life, relating to this sphere in *bhakta*, devotion and love. Crowley's *Liber Astarte vel Berylli* is certainly worth reading in this connection, and the following is one small quotation from this devotional text to elicit the full flavour of *bhakta* and *Netzach*.

> Let the devotee consider well that although Christ and Osiris be one, yet the former is to be worshipped with Christians, and the latter with Egyptian, rites. And this, although the rites themselves are ceremonially equivalent. There should, however, be *one* symbol declaring the transcending of such limitations; and with regard to the Deity also, there should be some one affirmation of his identity both with all other similar gods of other nations, and with the Supreme of whom all are but partial reflections.
>
> *Concerning the chief place of devotion*: This is the Heart of the Devotee, and should be symbolically represented by that room or spot which he loves best. And the dearest spot therein shall be the shrine of his temple. It is most convenient if this shrine and altar should be sequestered in woods, or in a private grove, or garden. But let it be protected from the profane.
>
> *Concerning the Image of the Deity*: Let there be an image of the Deity; first because in meditation there is mindfulness induced thereby; and second because a certain power enters and inhabits it by virtue of the ceremonies; or so it is said, and we deny it not. Let this image be the most beautiful and perfect which the devotee is able to procure; or if he be able to paint or to carve the same, it is all the better.

As for Deities with whose nature no Image is compatible, let them be worshipped in an empty shrine...

Concerning the Ceremonies: Let the Philosophus prepare a powerful Invocation of the particular Deity according to his Ingenium. But let it consist of these several parts:

First, an Imprecation, as of a slave unto his Lord.

Second, an Oath, as of a vassal to his Liege.

Third, a Memorial, as of a child to his Parent.

Fourth, an Orison, as of a Priest unto his God.

Fifth, a Colloquy, as of a Brother with his Brother.

Sixth, a Conjuration, as to a Friend with his Friend.

Seventh, a Madrigal, as of a Lover to his Mistress.

And mark well that the first should be of awe, the second of fealty, the third of dependence, the fourth of adoration, the fifth of confidence, the sixth of comradeship, the seventh of passion.

This is the essential spirit of *Netzach*.

HOD

Hod, is Glory, and in this eighth file we have all the mercurial gods, stressing the notion that here we have the mental and intellectual. It has a watery attribution, reflected from *Chesed*, so that there is a well-defined connection between Jupiter, the so-called higher mind, and Mercury, lower or the concrete forms of mental activity. Some of the modern writers consider Hod as a 'form' *Sepirah* as opposed to the 'force' concept of *Netzach*. It is the area of mental images on the inner plane and intellectual effort.

If we take the ancient phrase 'God geometrizes' and then add 'God philosophizes' we have something implied of the nature of *Hod*. Its attribution to Mercury is further indicative of its essential nature, for like the metal mercury, this phase of mental activity in man is eternally in a flux, never still for a moment. The description of the Roman and Greek Mercury is eloquent in describing the area of mental activity implied by *Hod*. A mythological dictionary asserts that Hermes was the god of commerce, wealth and good fortune as well as the messenger or herald of the gods. He seems also to have been the patron deity of tricksters, travellers, glib talkers and thieves. In early Greek history, he was also known as a fertility god, and interestingly enough, crude phallic images of him called *hermae* were set up at crossroads and in front of houses. Like the Egyptian Anubis, the dog-headed watcher of the temples, he was considered to be a psychopomp, the conductor of departed souls through the after-death states.

The magickal image is said to be a hermaphrodite. The name also used was Hermanubis, a combination of Hermes of the Greeks and Anubis of the Egyptians. The hermaphrodite or bi-sexual implies that Mercury or *Hod* is the area of thought-forms and is largely neutral and sexless; or let us say that its polarity is larval, depending upon the use to which these forms can be put by the ensouling emotional factors.

The divine name is *Elohim Tzabaoth*, the God of Hosts– the *Elohim*, let us recall from an earlier page, being in Hebrew the male plural termination of the singular female 'god'. This is opposed to *YHVH Tzabaoth* of *Netzach*, which is Johovah of Hosts or Armies. The archangel is said to be Michael, who is like God, and then we have to recall that of all the planets

Mercury is that which is nearest the sun and reflects the light of the sun more clearly than any other planet or satellite.

Just as the practical approach of *Netzach* is *bhakta*, so the *Hod* approach is *gnana*, philosophy. It is worthy to note that in Crowley's reformulation of the Golden Dawn, the specific tasks he prescribed for the grade attributed to Hod were the mastery of philosophy and above all of the Qabalah itself. Emphasis was directed for example to its mathematical parts so that any number might be fully investigated and understood in terms of its intrinsic formula.

Appropriately, there is in Dion Fortune's book this statement:

> If we have no magical capacity, which is the work of the intellectual imagination, the Sphere of *Hod* will be a closed book to us. We can only operate in a Sphere after we have received the initiation of that Sphere, which, in the language of the Mysteries, confers its powers. In the technical working of the Mysteries these initiations are conferred on the physical plane by means of ceremonial, which may be effectual, or may not. The gist of the matter lies in the fact that one cannot waken into activity that which is not already latent. Life is the real initiator; the experiences of life stimulate into function the capacities of our temperaments in such degree as we possess them. The ceremony of initiation, and the teachings that should be given in the various grades, are simply designed to make conscious what was previously subconscious, and to bring under the control of the will, directed by the higher intelligence, those developed reaction-capacities which have hitherto only responded blindly to their appropriate stimuli.

YESOD

Yesod, the Foundation, is the area of the lunar gods and those who preside over fertility, animal or vegetative. It is also the area of sex, so that without effort, this part of the filing cabinet can become extensive. Its magical image is that of a very strong naked man, capable of bearing large and heavy burdens–classically, Atlas holding the world on his shoulders. The Egyptian one is not dissimilar–Shu, the god of the air, who separates the sky-goddess Nuit from Geb, the god of the earth. Just to round out the symbolism, there is, paradoxically, the notion of the fundamental three phases of the moon, their deity attributions, and their functions in women. There is Artemis, or Selene, the young virginal goddess, huntress, chaste, innocent and pure–the moon in the opening days of her cycle. This is followed by the full moon, representing the fecund and fertile Mother, in full production as it were, fulfilling herself joyously in her basic generative function, symbolized by Aphrodite. This is the fertile and, because fulfilled, loved and loving woman in her prime. Then follows the moon in her decline, the waning moon, Hecate, the post-menopausal woman who has found no substitute fulfilment now that her child-bearing days are gone, she resents the loss of love and loving now that her sexual attractiveness has vanished, becoming embittered, sullen, skinny, and hag-like. This old crone who has no family, feared and hated because of her sharp masculinized tongue, was in old times suspected of witchcraft, and became altogether isolated.

Robert Graves expresses this extraordinarily well in the Introduction to his book *The Greek Myths:*

Since the sun's annual course similarly recalled the rise and decline of her physical powers–spring a maiden, summer a nymph, winter a crone–a goddess became identified with seasonal changes in animal and plant life; and thus with Mother Earth who, at the beginning of the vegetative year, produces only leaves and buds, then flowers and fruits, and at last ceases to bear. She could later be conceived as yet another triad; the maiden of the upper air, the nymph of the earth or sea, the crone of the underworld–typified by Selene, Aphrodite, and Hecate. These mystical analogues fostered the sacredness of the number three, and the Moon-goddess became enlarged to nine when each of the three persons–maiden, nymph, and crone–appeared in triad to demonstrate her divinity. Her devotees never quite forget that there were not three goddesses, but one goddess.

We are dealing with the generative power of nature which coordinates, integrates and stimulates the chemistry of our bodies, and the larger body of the earth we live on, and the chemistry of the solar and stellar systems in which we live. It is not a product of physical life, though it may seem to be so. It is, however, the power behind the scenes, as it were, activating the molecules, cells and tissues. Thus, it led to the concept of a hidden area behind or within nature which is the electro-magnetic model or energy-field shaping the protoplasm within that field. So that we have the theory of the etheric or astral world which preserves the stability of the material world and provides the invisible models for all things here below that can only be changed by altering the invisible astral fields and images. Modern notions of radiant energy are held referable here.

The divine name is *Shaddai El Chai*, Almighty Living God, the lord of generation, the indwelling divinity of the pelvis. The archangel is said to be Gabriel, the might of God who oversees the angels, who are the *Ishim*, the flames referred to in Psalms, 104:4.

Its element is air, and this The Tree of Life depicts as reflected down the middle pillar from *Kether* to *Tipareth*, and thence to *Yesod*, the sphere of generation. About this topic, Dion Fortune wrote some years ago:

> In dealing with the rhythms of Luna we are dealing with etheric, not physical conditions. The magnetism of living creatures waxes and wanes with a definite tide. It is a thing that is not difficult to observe when one knows what to look for. It shows itself most clearly in relations between persons in whom magnetism is fairly evenly balanced. Sometimes one will be in the ascendant, and sometimes the other.
>
> Now, it may be asked, if the Sphere of *Yesod* is etheric, why are the generative organs assigned to this sphere, for surely their function is physical, if anything is? The answer to that question is to be found in the knowledge of the subtler aspects of sex which appears to be entirely lost to the Western world…We must liken it to an iceberg, five-sixths of whose bulk is below the surface. The actual physical reactions of sex form a very small proportion, and by no means the most vital portion of its functioning.

MALKUTH

Malkuth, the Kingdom, is the tenth and final emanation in our filing system, the inferior representative of *Binah,* and in the *Zohar* she is called the Lower or Inferior Mother, *Malkah* the Queen and *Kallah* the Bride of Tetragrammaton.

Some of the symbols speak of *Malkuth* as a gate, the Gate of Death, the Gate of Tears, and even the Gate of the Daughter of the Mighty Ones. Some of these are drawn from the beautiful and sonorous titles given to the Tarot Cards. *Malkuth* is not a closed sphere; it leads always to the higher or interior *Sephiroth;* the gate is always open if we can but see it. She is also called 'The Virgin of the World', and some of the alchemical documents describe her, as the first matter of the Great Work, in some detail.

The divine Name is *Adonai ha-Aretz*, Lord of the Earth and its archangel is Sandalphon, and its choir of angels are said to be the Kerubim, the rulers of the elements. Above all other things it is the realm of the element earth, though the conventional charts of The Tree of Life split up the sphere of *Malkuth* into areas representing the four elements themselves. This *Sephirah* on The Tree symbolizes matter, the material world itself.

As Dr. Westcott wrote:

> The Kabalah teaches that one must entirely relinquish the apparent knowledge of matter as an entity apart from spirit. The assertion that matter exists, and is an entity entirely different from Spirit, and that Spirit–The God of Spirits– created it, must be denied, and the notion must be torn out

by the roots before progress can be made. If matter exists it is something, and must have come from something; but Spirit is not a thing, and creative Spirit, the highest Spiritual conception, could not make matter, the lowest things, out of nothing; hence it is not made, and hence there is no matter. All is Spirit and conception. *Ex nihilo nihil fit*. All that does exist can only have come from Spirit, from Divine Essence. That Being should arise from non-being is impossible. That matter should create itself is absurd; matter cannot proceed from Spirit; the two ideas are entirely apart; then matter cannot exist. Hence it follows that what we call matter is but an aspect, a conception, an illusion, a mode of motion, a delusion of our physical senses.

This is what Korzybski, the general semanticist, would have called the outmoded Aristotelian kind of thinking. A modern mystic, Vitvan, has attempted to conjoin general semantics or non-Aristotelian thought with the ancient wisdom, and have formulated some fascinating and highly creative concepts. Basic to his assumptions is the notion of identity– 'identification of images appearing substantive in an individual's psychic nature, with that from which stimuli (energy wave-lengths and frequencies) are received.'

Here is the great value in *conscious* abstracting, because by this process one learns to differentiate between an image-in-the-psychic-nature and configurations of units of energy constituting this world. ('Forms' was Plato's name for these we call configurations.)

As an image appears on the photographic plate in a camera, so energy wave-lengths and frequencies are formulated as a picture in the mental functions of an individual's psychic nature. When this picture, due to the various neural and brain processes, *appears 'out there'*, i.e., substantive, it becomes identified with a given configuration of unit of energy from which stimuli are received, then that image-appearing-substantive in the psychic nature becomes designated, labeled, etc., 'a thing', 'object', etc...

In the totality, this formulation of qualities into mental images, constitutes what we call 'the objective world'. This identification and belief therein represents what we call 'the error'.

This intellectual error that Vitvan refers to is prevalent in many metaphysical systems including Christian Science as well as Vedanta–the delusion of matter, the notion that the world is Maya as the Orientals would say. It is also stressed in Westcott's interpretation of the non-existence of matter, due no doubt to his having been considerably influenced by association with Madame H.P. Blavatsky and the Eastern School of esotericism.

Be that as it may, the important notion to be derive from this is that *Malkuth*, the tenth *Sephirah*, is the Divine Kingdom. The world we inhabit is a divine world, and it is only due to the spiritual fog we live in, the blindness of our minds due to the limitations of our sensory systems, that we fail to perceive it as the living body of God. Only children, lovers, many artists–poets, painters and writers–an mystics have been able to see *Malkuth* as it really is, and not as a dead, empty shell. They see it, as did Thomas Traherne, who reported his vision of reality in *Centuries of Meditation*:

> The corn was orient and immortal wheat, which never should be reaped, nor was ever sown. I thought it had stood from everlasting to everlasting. The dust and the stones of the street were as precious as gold; the gates were at first the end of the world. The green trees when I saw them first through one of the gates, transported and ravished me, their sweetness and unusual beauty made my heart to leap, and almost mad with ecstasy, they were such strange and wonderful things. The men! O what venerable and reverend creatures did the aged seem! Immortal Cherubim! and the young men glittering and sparkling angels, and maids, strange seraphic pieces of life and beauty. Boys and girls tumbling in the street, and playing, were moving jewels...I know not that they were born or should die. But all things abided eternally as they were in their proper places. Eternity was manifest in the Light of the Day, and something infinite behind everything appeared.

To complete this simple discussion of the Tree of Life, I can think of nothing more fitting than Paul F. Case's 'Pattern on the Trestleboard'. It has a distinct metaphysical flavour, since there has been in the United States a well-defined interplay between the metaphysical and occult movements. In this particular instance I think both may have profited.

THE PATTERN ON THE TRESTLEBOARD

This is the Truth about the Self.

0. All the power that ever was or will be is here now.

1. I am a centre of expression for the Primal Will-to-Good which eternally creates and sustains the universe.

2. Through me its unfailing Wisdom takes form in thought and word.

3. Filled with Understanding of its perfect law, I am guided, moment by moment, along the path of liberation.

4. From the exhaustless riches of its Limitless Substance, I draw all things needful, both spiritual and material.

5. I recognize the manifestation of the undeviating Justice in all the circumstances of my life.

6. In all things, great and small, I see the Beauty of the divine expression.

7. Living from that Will, supported by its unfailing Wisdom and Understanding, mine is the Victorious Life.

8. I look forward with confidence to the perfect realization of the Eternal Splendour of the Limitless Light.

9. In thought and deed, I rest my life, from day to day, upon the sure Foundation of Eternal Being.

10. The Kingdom of Spirit is embodied in my flesh.*

---

*For kind permission to quote this 'Pattern on the Trestleboard' I must acknowledge the generosity of Mrs. Harriet Case, the widow of the late Paul F. Case (founder of the B.O.T.A.)

FURTHER READING

Once the student has learned to feel at home intellectually with these elementary Qabalistic concepts and can function to some extent with them, he will then be ready to turn his attention to some of the more serious or more comprehensive texts.

In the order given, I strongly recommend the following for further reading:

1. *Introduction to the Kaballah*, William Wynn Westcott.
2. *The Kaballah*, Christian D. Ginsburg.
3. *The Mystical Qabalah*, Dion Fortune.
4. *Practical Course in Qabalistic Symbolism*, Gareth Knight.
5. *Liber 777*, Aleister Crowley.
6. *Kaballah Unveiled*, Introduction by MacGregor Mathers.
7. *The Secret Doctrine in Israel*, A.E. Waite.
8. *Sepher Yetzirah*, Translated by William Wynn Westcott.
9. *On the Kaballah and its Symbolism*, G.G. Scholem.
10. *Apocalypse Unveiled*, James Pryse.
11. *The Tarot*, Paul F. Case.
12. *The Seven Rays of Q.B.L.*, Frater Albertus Spagyricus, (Paracelsus Research Society, Salt Lake City, 1968).

Chapter 3

THE QABALAH OF NUMBER AND MEANING

*An Elementary Manual of
Numerical Procedures*

When I was about sixteen years of age, I first became interested enough in the Qabalah to read voraciously what little of it was available at that time in English. It was surprisingly diminutive in quantity and quality.

Since I then resided in Washington, D.C., I made the Library of Congress my second home. I derived a great deal of pleasure browsing, not only through the extensive files but, after obtaining permission, through the vast stacks also. In due course of time, I had made the acquaintance of the scholarly head of the Semitic Division of the Library and, as though I were free-associating to him, made mention of a burning ambition. When I knew enough, I wanted to be able to translate into English several of the ancient texts that still remained in Hebrew and Aramaic. He was wise enough to recommend to me a Hebrew tutor. This was a young man attending college in Washington who needed some extra funds to facilitate his staying in the city.

Every week, then, for about a year I received a lesson from him. Gradually I learned to read Hebrew fairly fluently, to understand some of the fundamentals of its complex grammar and syntax, and, if the material was sufficiently elementary, to translate it into English passably well. I never persevered long enough to learn to speak the language–which today I regret very much.

But the major result of that year's tutorship was this: though I never succeeded in fulfilling my adolescent dream to translate Qabalistic texts into English, I did manage to acquire a solid foundation of the language which has stood me in good stead where some Qabalistic fundamentals were concerned.

Gematria, for example, really presents no problem. This I attribute entirely to the linguistic education given me by my tutor, and the same is true for other phases of the so-called practical Qabalah.

No by this I do not wish to imply that every student should take a year of Hebrew grammar and reading in order to understand some of the Qabalistic methods of elucidation of hidden facets of meaning in the names and symbols of the Old Testament; or to enable him intelligently to construct talismans and amulets in that branch of Qabalah that is known as Theurgy. This is not altogether necessary.

But it may be worthwhile pointing out that great advantage may be obtained from a little study of the Hebrew alphabet, and from some slight experience in drawing and painting these letters as the magical symbols they really are, as well as from familiarizing oneself with certain basic Hebrew words relative to the *Sephiroth* on The Tree of Life. All this would render intelligible numbers of facts which even otherwise astute writers and students of the Qabalah are inclined to gloss over, dismissing them as wholly unimportant to the subject.

SIMPLE GEMATRIA

A few very simple examples should rapidly convey the kind of hidden meaning sought by the Qabalists in their apparently arbitrary manipulation of words, letters and numbers.

For instance, there is the Hebrew word *Achad*. It means 'one' or 'unity'. Its spelling is:

Aleph + *Cheth* + *Daleth*
1 + 8 + 4

Its numerical total or value, or Gematria, thus is thirteen, 13. It so happens that there is another Hebrew word *ahavah*– meaning 'love'. It is spelt:

Aleph + *Heh* + *Beth* + *Heh*
1 + 5 + 2 + 5

Its numerical value is also thirteen, as is the preceding word. Thus it is assumed that, since they have identical number values, there is a connection between love and unity–one leading into and producing the other. I can never think of this matter without recalling St. Paul's definition of charity or love:

> Though I speak with the tongues of men and angels, and have not charity, I am become as sounding brass, or a tinkling cymbal…Charity suffereth long, and is kind; charity

envieth not; charity vaunteth not itself, is not puffed up, doth not behave itself unseemly, seeketh not her own, is not easily provoked, thinketh no evil, rejoiceth not in iniquity, but rejoiceth in the truth; beareth all things, believeth all things, hopeth all things, endureth all things. Charity never faileth; but whether there be prophecies, they shall fail, whether there be tongues, they shall cease; whether there be knowledge, it shall vanish away. For we know in part, and we prophesy in part. But when that which is perfect is come, then that which is in part shall be done away... And now abideth faith, hope, charity, these three; but the greatest of these is charity.

If we join the numbers of love and unity together, uniting them as it were, the product becomes 26. This is the numerical value of the Tetragrammaton, the four-lettered name of God:

$$\underset{10}{Yod} + \underset{5}{Heh} + \underset{6}{Vau} + \underset{5}{Heh} = 26$$

From this operation, the Qabalists therefore deduce that God, who is One and only One, operates through love, and that His nature may well be defined as unity and love conjoined. Or, that He is a unity operating through duality to produce love.

Incidentally, it is worth mentioning that there are two valuable aids for the student who is attempting to become adept in the use of these methods. The first is a Hebrew-English and English-Hebrew Dictionary which he can consult for the meanings of words developed through Gematria. The second is an even more valuable book. It is *Sepher Sephiroth* to be found in *Equinox VIII*. This is a large book originally begun by Frater Iehi Aour (Allan Bennett) of the Golden Dawn, and then continued and completed by Aleister Crowley who became his *chela*, in the early years of the century.

This book consists of a large number of Hebrew words extrapolated both from the Scriptures and from some of the original Qabalistic texts–particularly parts of the *Zohar* and the *Sepher Yetzirah*. The Gematria of several hundreds of words and names have been carefully worked out by these two Qabalists, who then classified each word according to its number. So that if in the course of study one has developed a significant number, it is then possible to look it up in *Sepher Sephiroth* in order to ascertain what other words or names have been gathered together with that particular number.

The more skill one develops in using the Qabalah of numbers and meaning, the more useful this book becomes. It is really a dictionary of Qabalistic numbers. it has been republished in *The Qabalah of Aleister Crowley*, (N.Y. Weiser and Co., 1973).

(See chart on page 92.)

NOTARIQON

In a quite different direction, there is a method called Notariqon, which is a Hebrew word meaning shorthand writing. It consists in making neologisms (new words) from the initial letters of certain selected words.

In alchemical literature, there is a famous example of the use of Notariqon. Take the word vitriol, which is sulphur. Each letter of this word becomes the initial of another word forming a sentence of seven words:

	Name in Hebrew	Meaning of Letter	English Letter	Numeration	Sepher Yetzirah	Tarot
1.	*Aleph*	Ox	A	1		0 - Fool
2.	*Beth*	House	B	2	Mercury	I - Magician
3.	*Gimel*	Camel	G	3	Moon	II - High Priestess
4.	*Daleth*	Door	D	4	Venus	III - Empress
5.	*Heh*	Window	H	5	Aries	IV - Emperor
6.	*Vau*	Nail	V	6	Taurus	V - Hierophant
7.	*Zayin*	Sword	Z	7	Gemini	VI - Lovers
8.	*Cheth*	Fence	Ch	8	Cancer	VII - Chariot
9.	*Teth*	Serpent	T	9	Leo	VIII - Strength
10.	*Yod*	Finger	I, J, Y	10	Virgo	IX - Hermit
11.	*Caph*	Palm of Hand	K	20	Jupiter	X - Wheel of Fortune
12.	*Lamed*	Whip	L	30	Libra	XI - Justice
13.	*Mem*	Water	M	40	Water	XII - Hanged Man
14.	*Nun*	Fish	N	50	Scorpio	XIII - Death
15.	*Samech*	Arrow	S	60	Sagittarius	XIV - Temperance
16.	*Ayun*	Eye	NG	70	Capricorn	XV - Devil
17.	*Peh*	Mouth	P	80	Mars	XVI - Blasted Tower
18.	*Tzaddi*	Hook	TZ	90	Aquarius	XVII - Star
19.	*Qoph*	Back of Head	Q	100	Pisces	XVIII - The Moon
20.	*Resh*	Head	R	200	Sun	XIX - The Sun
21.	*Shin*	Tooth	Sh	300	Fire	XX - Judgment
22.	*Tau*	Cross	T	400	Saturn	XXI - The World

V Visita
I Interiora
T Terrae
R Rectificando
I Invenies
O Occultum
L Labidem

The entire sentence, the, which is an expension of vitriol, carries with it the meaning of 'Visit or explore the interior or depths of the Earth, and find and rectify the secret Stone.'

One of the traditional names for the Qabalah is the *Chokmah Nestorah*, the Secret Wisdom. It is considered to be that esoteric knowledge which has been handed down from time immemorial. By taking the first letter of these two words, *Cheth* and *Nun*, and combining them, the result is a word pronounced *chen*. By consulting a Hebrew lexicon, it will be discovered that there is a legitimate word *chen* which means grace. Hence the Qabalists argued that when it is mentioned in holy script that God vouchsafed His grace to so-and-so, the hidden interpretation is that he transmitted the secret esoteric knowledge of the divine life and plan. This was His grace.

THE NOTARIQON OF THE TENACH

An even more common and prosaic example of this method is in daily use among the Jewish people, though it is strongly to be doubted if many of them recognize it as a traditional method of Qabalistic exegesis. In Hebrew, the Bible–the Old Testament– is named the *Tenach* (always remember the 'ch' in Hebrew is a gutteral pronunciation, as in the Scottish word 'loch'). It is spelled *Tau, Nun* and final *Caph*.

This is really a notariqon, or a neologism, based upon three Hebrew words:

Torah —the first few books of the Bible, the so-called Five Books of Moses.

N'vee-im —the books of the Prophets, several texts including Isaiah, Jeremiah, etc.

K'soovim —the Holy Writings; the miscellaneous, group of scriptures comprised of the Psalms, Proverbs, Ecclesiastes, *et al*.

The first letter of each of these three words is extracted and used to form a new word *Tenach*. This word is, in effect, a shorthand abbreviation to represent the contents of the whole of the Old Testament.

THE GEMATRIA OF 'AMEN'

Another very common word, used by Jews and all Christian denominations alike, without very much insight or understanding, is the word 'Amen'. Its origins and meaning are quite obscure. Its use at the close of a prayer is generally considered to imply 'Let it be so!' or 'So mote it be!' The Qabalists, however, give it an interpretation which is a particular exhortation of divinity. Its letters, *Aleph, Mem, Nun*, are considered to be the initials of the three Hebrew words relating to God.

Aleph = the first letter of *Adonai*, my Lord.

Mem = the first letter of *Melekh*, King.

Nun = the first letter of *Na'amon*, Faithful.

The whole meaning of 'Amen', the, is 'Lord, Faithful King'. The peroration is thus simultaneously a divine invocation.

If we wished to pursue this further, we could determine the Gematria of 'Amen', which is:

$$\left. \begin{array}{l} Aleph = 1 \\ Mem = 40 \\ Nun = 50 \end{array} \right\} = 91.$$

There are a number of other Hebrew words in *Sepher Sephiroth* having this same number. Somehow an intimate connection would have to be established between them. *Ehlon* (*Aleph, Yog, Lamed, Nun*) is a tree. The biblical word *Ephod* (*Aleph, Peh, Daleth*) meaning the coloured garment worn by the high priest, has also the same number. *Malkah* (*Mem, Lamed, Caph, Aleph*) a virgin or a bride, as well as *Manna* (*Mem, Nun, Aleph*) are still further examples of this number. Connections between these words and numbers may appear obscure at first, but the wise experienced Qabalist could readily trace them out. In reality, a species of free association is used.

There is one final manipulation of 'Amen' and its numerical value of 91. These two digits may be added together by so-called theosophical addition to produce 10. Ten is the number on the Tree of Life of *Malkuth*, the Kingdom, the last of the holy emanations from God, the completion of the chain of numbers, and by the elimination of the zero, the beginning of another sequence of numbers and ideas.

'RUACH ELOHIM'

Finally, there is the example of *Ruach Elohim*, two Hebrew words mentioned in the opening verses of Genesis referring to the Spirit of God brooding over the waters of creation. A more literal rendition would really be 'The Spirit of the God'. The

Gematria of these two words joined together in 300, demonstrated as follows:

$Ruach =$ $Resh + Vau + Cheth$
$200 + 6 + 8 = 214$

$Elohim =$ $Aleph + Lamed + Heh + Yod + Mem$
$1 + 30 + 5 + 10 + 40 = 86$

Added together they yield 300. (By lopping off the two zeros, this number could be reduced to 3, and 3 is the path of *Gimel*, the Camel, attributed to the Tarot card The High Priestess, who has the title of Priestess of the Silver Star–the path descending from *Kether* above to *Tiphareth* below.)

The letter *Shin*–a three pronged letter–was considered to be the equivalent of these two words, not merely because of the identity of their numbers (which would be enough), but because *Shin* in the *Sepher Yetzirah* was attributed to the element of fire. In many areas of the Old Testament, fire is considered an attribute of God, indicative of His presence. Later, light became one of these attributes–light and fire being interrelated and interconnected. Thus, one of the old magickal exercises associated with visualizing the descent of divine spirit was to use a concrete symbol–a large fiery red letter *Shin*, imagined above the head. In this connection, I never fail to think of the peroration of one of Crowley's earliest essays:

> Under the stars will I go forth, my brothers, and drink of that lustral dew; I will return my brothers, when I have seen God face to face, and read within those eternal eyes the secret that shall make you free...

Thus shall we give back its youth to the world, for like *tongues of triple flame* we shall brood upon the Great Deep–Hail unto the Lords of the Groves of Eleusis! (my italics)

One of the early traditions has it that when God uttered *Fiat Lux*, 'Let there be light', he commanded not merely the physical appearance of light and all that it entails, but, so states the ancient wisdom, the emergence of the divine mystery. For light is *Aour* (*Aleph, Vau, Res* = 207) and *Raz*, (*Resh, Zayin* =207) meaning mystery.

Thus light in all its manifold significances *is* the divine mystery.

The Qabalist catches glimpses of this mythos in his magical or theurgic working, of a ray of the infinite light.

Zohar means radiance or splendour; thus another reference to light. The radiance of the divine light is reflected in the mysteries of the text of this Qabalistic work. But when these mysteries are cloaked in merely literal theological interpretation, this splendour is obscured and hidden. The literal prosaic meaning was always considered by mystics to be but darkness and obscurity. The esoteric interpretations elicit the *Raz* or mystery as well as the *Zohar* or Splendrous Light that many believe to shine through every line of the sacred scriptures.

Ain Soph Aour is the infinite Light from which the *Sephiroth* of The Tree of Life have emanated. Thus the light is also, in many more ways than one, the great mystery without end.

PARADISE

There is a good deal of symbolic 'play' with the Hebrew word for paradise–*pardes*, meaning also a garden. Some of the early Qabalists related its letters *Peh, Resh, Daleth, Samech* to the four rivers that in Genesis are said to flow forth from the Garden of Eden. For example in the *Golden Dawn*, one of the early rituals contained the following references:

> The River *Naher* (meaning never-failing waters) flows forth from the Supernal Eden and in *Daath* it is divided into four heads:
>
> *Pison*: Fire–flowing to *Geburah* where there is Gold.
>
> *Gihon*: Water–the Waters of Mercy, flowing into *Chesed*.
>
> *Hiddikel*: Air–flowing into *Tiphareth*.
>
> *Phrath*: (Euphrates): *Malkuth* ...The River going out of Eden is the River of the Apocalypse, the Waters of Life, clear as crystal proceeding from the Throne, on either side of the Tree of Life, bearing all manner of fruit.

Now compare this set of bare occult dogmas relative to the elements to a far earlier Qabalistic interpretation in which these letters and the Rives are compared to levels of meaning:

1. *Peh* for *Pison* = literal meaning (*Peshat*).

2. *Resh* for *Remez* = allegorical meaning, and the River *Gihon*.

3. *Daleth* for *Derasha* = talmudic (the sharp and deft) interpretation, and for *Hiddikel*.

4. *Samech* for *Sod* = mystical and innermost meaning, and for *Phrath*.

So that the wisdom derived from not one but multiple levels of meaning and interpretation lead, as it were, to paradise, to illumination.

NAMES OF GOD

There is a page or so from Francis Barrett's *Magus*, the section on Ceremonial Magic, that is of some consequence here. This book, originally published circa 1800, is a hotch-potch of superstitious nonsense and some basic magical information, in about equal proportions. New editions of this book are now available, (*The Magus*, Thorsons 1977.) The serious student could do far worse than to obtain a copy, so long as he learns to separate the wheat from the chaff which is copiously and abundantly present. Some of this quotation throws a great deal of light on many of the strange-appearing, almost Hebrew names appearing in some of the old invocations.

The Hebrew in this text is appalling. I imagine many of those mistakes have been inadvertently perpetuated by ignorant copyists. Names are copied by students who knew little or no Hebrew so that after the original copy has passed through a dozen illiterate hands, and undergone as many alterations and mutilations, the final project bears little resemblance to any accurate original, and is to all intents and purposes indecipherable.

I say this phenomenon within the confines of the Golden Dawn. Some of the students must have copied the Hebrew letters from original manuscripts without any insight or understanding. Their inaccuracies and miscopyings have been perpetuated right down the line to this day. Perhaps it may be said that this makes little difference. But it does imply ignorance above all. And when the making and drawing of all talismans are considered, the Hebrew mistakes are seen in specimens repeated by Barrett and in some old grimoires, are so appalling as to make the talisman meaningless. It would be just as effective (or useless, as the case may be) to inscribe hieroglyphs and lines drawn at random instead of Hebrew letters and sigils.

Instances of this type indicate strongly that the elementary study of basic Hebrew should be made mandatory in whatever sanctuaries of initiation still exist so that, if they teach the Qabalah, the monstrous illiterate errors of former times may never again be repeated.

'God himself, though he be one only essence,' wrote Barrett in section of his book referred to above, 'yet hath divers names, which expound not his divers essences or deities; but certain properties flowing down from him; by which names he pours down upon us and all his creatures, many benefits…'

In some of the following examples given by Barrett, I have taken the liberty of eliminating the Hebrew letters and making the appropriate corrections in his transliteration into English.

'*Hua* is another name revealed to Esau, signifying the abyss of Godhead…' This word means simply 'He', and is attributed to *Kether*. '*Esch* is another name received from Moses, which soundeth fire, and is the name of God' *Na* is to be invocated in perturbations and troubles. There is also the name *Yah*, and the name *Elion* (which translated "the most high"), and the name *Macom* (this word means "place"), the name *Caphu*…'

Barrett spells this name *Caphu* with a *Caph*, *Peh*, and *Beth* which is quite meaningless. I can only assume that the *Beth* was a copyist's mistake for a *Resh*, in which case we would find *Capur* or *Kippur*, meaning 'atonement'. '…and the name *Innon*, and the name *Emeth*, which is interpreted truth, and is the seal of God; and there are two other names *Tzur* ("Rock") and *Aben*, ("stone"), both of these signify a solid work, and one of them expressed the Father with the Son; and many names we have placed in the scale of numbers...' Barrett then mentions the arts of Notariqon and Gematria by means of which words and numbers are derived, and proceeds:

> In like manner the name Iaia, from this verse: *YHVH Aloheu YHVH Achod*, this is, God our God is One God. [In reality it is to be translated, 'Jehovah, our God, Jehovah is One.'] In like manner the name *IaVa*, from this verse: *Iehi Aour, vayehi Aour*, that is 'Let there be Light and there was light'...and his name *Hacaba* is extracted from this verse, *Ha-Qadesh baruch hua* ('the Holy One, blessed be He')... These sacred words have not their power in magical operations from themselves, as they are words, but from the occult divine powers working by them in the minds of those who by faith adhere to them.

AGLA and ARARITA

I have omitted a direct quotation from Barrett dealing with two classical words found commonly in some of the older magical rituals because they deserve a somewhat fuller consideration. In the banishing ritual of the Pentagram, now to be found in many publications, there is a four-lettered word AGLA. This is another good example of a notariqon, and its analysis is really quite simple. There are four words from the Scriptures meaning 'Thou art mighty for ever, O Lord [Adonai].' In Hebrew, this phrase is *Atoh gibor l'olahm adonai*. The initials of these words placed together form AGLA.

There is an even more common ritual name which is more obscure (and which has often been miscopied atrociously), save to the rare good student. The magical name ARARITA is found particularly in the Hexagram Ritual, and is to be vibrated in each of the four quarters while tracing the appropriate geometrical figure with sigils. The six points and the centre of the Hexagram are attributed to the *forces* of the seven planets, which are thus invoked or banished by the correct use of this figure. It, too, is a fine example of a notariqon, and its seven letters are the initials of the following sentence: 'One is His beginning; One is His individuality; His permutation is One.' The corresponding Hebrew is: *Achad raysheethoh; achad Resh Yechidathoh; Temurathoh achod.*

The word *Achad* means 'one'; we have examined this word several times so far. *Raysheeh* is the Hebrew word for beginning, and the addition of the suffix 'oh' merely means 'His'. *Resh* means a head or a beginning, and is the root of *Raysheeth*. Qabalistic students will remember the word *Yechidah* as being attributed to *Kether*, representing, when dealing with the constitution of man the Individual, the immortal part of man. So that the phrase *Resh Yechidathoh* means the Head of his Individuality. *Temurah* means permutation; the 'oh' on the end meaning 'His'. Thus is resolved this otherwise highly complex and confusing Hebrew sentence which yields the magical name ARARITA.

A very interesting example of this exegetical process is to be found in *The Golden Dawn*, Vol. I, p. 166, probably contributed to S.L. MacGregor Mathers:

> Here is a method of writing Hebrew words by the Yetziratic attribution of the alphabet, whence results some curious hieroglyphic symbolism. Thus Tetragrammaton will be written Virgo, Aries, Taurus, Aries. *Eheieh*, by Air, Aires, Virgo, Aries. From *Yeheshuah*, the Qabalistic mode of spelling Jesus, which is simply the Tetragrammaton with the letter *Shin* placed therein, we obtain a very peculiar combination–Virgo, Aires, Fire, Taurus, Aries. Virgo born of a Virgin, Aries the Sacrificial lamb, Fire the Fire of the

Holy Spirit, Taurus the Ox of the Earth in whose Manger He was laid, and lastly Aries the flocks of sheep whose Herdsmen came to worship Him. *Elohim* yields Aire, Libra, Aries, Virgo, Water–the Firmament, the Balanced Forces, the Fire of Spirit (for Aries is a fiery sign) operating in the Zodiac, the Fire Goddess, and the Waters of Creation.

A much longer and more complex demonstration of Qabalistic methods of elucidation, which elaborate at greater length these simpler techniques, is to be found in the following example. Though I have tried to render this demonstration as simple as I can, it still needs to be followed with some care and attention.

I.N.R.I.

Let us take as a start, an old application of Qabalistic principles–the English letters I.N.R.I. They are, of course, the initials of a Latin phrase once placed by the Romans at the head of the Cross representing the phrase 'Jesus of Nazareth, King of the Jews'. Several other theological meanings to these letters have been given at different periods of history by various groups of people and scholars.

For example, the mediaeval alchemists suggested that I.N.R.I. meant 'Igne Natura Renovatur Integra'–the whole of Nature is renewed by fire.

Another example of about the same period elaborated the four letters to 'Igne Nitrum Raris Invenitum', translated as 'shining (or glittering) is rarely found in fire.'

The Jesuits in their day interpreted it as 'Justum Necare Regis Impius': 'It is just to kill an impious king.'

J.S.M. Ward in his book *Freemasonry and the Ancient Gods* gives another example:

I	*Yam* = Water
N	*Nour* = Fire
R	*Ruach* = Air
I	*Yebeshah* = Earth

Thus the four letters are Hebrew initials of the four ancient elements.

In the nineteenth century, when the Hermetic Order of the Golden Dawn came to be formed, these letters were picked up and integrated into the complex structure of the Order's symbolism. It was used as the keyword to one of its ritual grades, that of the Adeptus Minor. To follow the interpretation used by the Order we need only the most superficial knowledge of attributions given in the Sepher Yetzirah, the Tarot pack of cards, a smattering of Gnosticism and astrology. The first gesture is to convert the four letters into their Hebrew equivalents and then to their direct Yetziratic attributions, as follows:

I	*Yod*	= Virgo	= ♍
N	*Nun*	= Scorpio	= ♏
R	*Resh*	= Sun	= ☉
I	*Yod*	= Virgo	= ♍

The final 'I', being repetitious, is dropped, only to be picked up again in a later place in order to extend the significance of the meanings derived from the analysis.

This breakdown, is nonetheless highly suggestive. Elementary astrology will extend the meaning a little. Virgo represents the virginal sign of nature itself. Scorpio is the sign of death and transformation; sex is involved here as well. Sol, the sun, is the source of light and life to all on earth; it is the centre of our solar system. All the so-called resurrection gods are known to be connected with the sun. The sun was thought to die every winter when vegetation perished and the earth became cold and barren. Every spring, when the sun returned, green life was restored to the earth.

Then we could look at *Liber 777*, which codified most of the basic knowledge material of the Golden Dawn and added more as it was gradually acquired by its author, Aleister Crowley. In one of the columns of this book entitled 'Egyptian Gods' we find the following which we can add to the data already obtained.

Virgo = Isis – who was Nature, the Mother of all things.

Scorpio = Apophis – death, the destroyer.

Sol = Osiris – slain and risen, the Egyptian resurrection and vegetative God.

Here we begin to get a definite sequence of ideas that proves somewhat meaningful. The simplicity of a natural state of affairs in, shall we say, the Garden of Eden (representing the springtime of mankind) is shattered by the intrusion of the knowledge of Good and Evil, sexual perception. This is due to the intervention of the destroyer Apophis, or Lucifer the Lightbearer, who changed all things–by illuminating all things. Thus the Fall, as well as the fall of the year. This is succeeded by the advent of Osiris the resurrection God who stated 'This is my body, which I destroy in order that it may be renewed.' He is the symbolic prototype of the perfected Solar Man, who suffered through earthly experience, was glorified by trial, was betrayed and killed, and then rose again to renew all things.

The final analysis of the keyword sums up the formula with the initials of *I*sis, *A*pophis, *O*siris = IAO, the supreme god of Gnostics (IAO is pronounced ee-ah-oh).

Since the sun is the giver of life and light, the formula must refer to light as the redeemer. The Order of the Golden Dawn was predicated on the age-old process of bringing light to the natural man. In order words, it taught psycho-spiritual techniques leading to illumination, to enlightenment. In this connection, one should always remember those beautiful versicles about the light in the opening chapter of the Gospel according to St. John.

In the very first of Neophyte Ritual of the Golden Dawn, the candidate is startled to hear the strangely-worded invocation 'Khabs Am Pehkt. Konx om Pax. Light in Extension.' In other words, 'May you too receive the benediction of the light, and undergo the mystical experience, the goal of all our work.'

'The enlightenment by a ray of the divine light which transforms the psychic nature of man may be an article of faith,' says Hans Jonas in his excellent book *The Gnostic Religion*, 'but it may also be an experience...Annihilation and deification of the person are fused in the spiritual ecstasis which purports to experience the immediate presence of the acosmic essence.'

> In the gnostic context, this transfiguring face-to-face experience is *gnosis* in the most exalted and at the same time the most paradoxical sense of the term, since it is knowledge of the unknowable...The mystical *gnosis theôu*–direct beholding of the divine reality–is itself an earnest of the consummation to come. It is transcendence become immanent; and although prepared for by human acts of self-modification which induce the proper disposition, the event itself is one of divine activity and grace. It is thus as much a 'being known' by God as a 'knowing' Him, and in this ultimate mutuality the 'gnosis' is beyond the terms of 'knowledge' properly speaking.

Since this is the basic theme recurrent through all the Golden Dawn rituals and teaching, we would expect to find it repeated and expanded in the analysis of the keyword of the Adeptus Minor grade. And of course it is there, clearly defined.

The word light is translated into LVX, the Latin word for light. A series of physical mimes or gestures are made by the officiants to represent the descent of this light, as well as to summarize the symbolism of the previous findings.

So one Adept or officiant raises his right arm directly in the air above him, while extending his left arm straight outwards (as though to signal making a left turn when driving a car). This forms by shape the letter L.

A second Adept raises his arms as though in supplication above his head–the letter V.

The third Adept extends his arms outwards forming a cross.

All together finally cross their arms on their chests, forming the letter X.

(A single person may of course perform the identical gestures.)

In any event, the letters form LVX which is now interpreted as the Light of the Cross. It is so interpreted because the letters INRI were initially found on the Crucifix, and because LVX means light. Finally the letters LVX themselves are portions of one type or another of the Cross:

A process of repetition is followed in order to synthesize all these variegated ideas and gestures, and to add one more mime to replace the second 'I' that was eliminated for being repetitious.

As the L sign is being made, the Adept says: 'The Sign of the Mourning of Isis'. This expresses the sorrow of Isis on learning that Osiris had been slain by Set or Apophis.

As the V sign is made, the Adept says, 'The Sign of Apophis and Typhon'. These are the other names for Set, the brother and murderer of Osiris, whose body was so mutilated that only the phallus could be found by Isis who had searched all over creation for him.

As the Adept spreads his arms outward to the side forming actively the Cross, he says, 'The Sign of Osiris Slain'.

Then, crossing one arm over the other on the chest, he adds: 'And risen. Isis, Apophis, Osiris, IAO.'

Thus what started out to be a simple abbreviation of a traditional Latin sentence on the Cross above the head of Christ, has now evolved by a Qabalistic process of exegesis into a complex series of evocative ideas and symbolic gestures which extend tremendously the root idea. And by knowing these ideas, the gestures may be used practically to aspire to the illumination it suggests. This is the essential value of the sacramental actions.

The Rosicrucian equivalent of this formula is found in the *Fama Fraternitatis*, one of the original three classical Rosicrucian documents: 'Ex Deo Nascimur. In Jesu Morimur. Per spiritus sanctus reviviscimus.': 'From God are we born. In Christ we die. We are revived by the Holy Spirit.'

Nor is this all. If we take LVX as symbols of Roman numerals, we have 65. This number, therefore, attains the symbolic equivalent of light, gnosis and illumination.

The Adeptus Minor obligation imposed on the candidate during the ritual initiation obligates him to aspire and work and practice so that by enlightenment he may one day 'become more than human'. This is the Qabalistic philosophy summarized in the statement that the Adept seeks to unite himself to his higher soul or his higher self, symbolized again in the Hebrew word *Adonai*. All the above notions therefore are synthesized in this word *Adonai*, literally translated 'My lord'. Its Hebrew letters are:

$$\text{Aleph} + \text{Daleth} + \text{Nun} + \text{Yod}$$
$$1 + 4 + 50 + 10 = 65$$

This number is also that of LVX, light. Qabalistically, the process enables us to perceive a necessary connection between *Adonai* and the light–their identity.

SYMBOLISM OF THE HEART AND THE SERPENT

In 1907, when Aleister Crowley received some of his most meaningful illuminations after a decade of hard magical work and spiritual discipline, he wrote an inspirational book which he called *Liber LXV*, which we have seen is 65. Its sub-title was 'The Book of the Heart girt with a Serpent'. This latter phrase was extrapolated from the last section of an old ritual found in some scholarly texts entitled 'The Bornless Ritual'. its last paragraph reads:

I am He, the Bornless (or eternal) Spirit
Having Sight in the feet, strong and the Immortal Fire.
I am He, the Truth!
I am He who hate that evil should be wrought in the world!
I am He that lighteneth and thundereth!
I am He from whom is the shower of the Life of Earth!
I am He whose mouth ever flameth!
I am He, the Grace of the World!
The Heart girt with a serpent is my name.

It is the above underlined phrase which Crowley appropriated as the title of his illuminated book to bear witness to *Adonai*.

What of the symbols of the heart and the serpent? What meaning have they?

The heart has clear reference to the emotional life, to the inner core of man, to 'the heart of the matter', as we would colloquially say. And of the many titles given to Christ, one of them, 'The Sacred Heart', represents his passion, his sacrifice, and his redemptive love of mankind.

The serpent is an even more ancient and sophisticated symbol. It not only represents the abuse of the sexual force that corrupted and precipitated the Fall and expulsion from Eden, but also the transmuted and sublimated libido. Known as the *kundalini*, it is trained to arise out of the dark pelvic area, to course up the spine to form the golden aureole around the head of the saint or the fully enlightened adept.

> I am the Heart; and the Snake is entwined
> About the invisible core of the mind.
> Rise, O my snake! It is now the hour
> Of the hooded and holy ineffable flower.
> Rise, O my snake, into brilliance of bloom
> On the corpse of Osiris afloat in the tomb!
> O heart of my mother, my sister, mine, own,
> Thou art given to Nile, to the terror Typhon!
> Ah me! but the glory of ravening storm
> Enswathes thee and wraps thee in frenzy of form.
> Be still, O my soul! that the spell may dissolve
> As the wands are upraised, and the aeons revolve.
> Behold! We are one, and the tempest of years
> Goes down to the dusk, and the Beetle appears.
> Oh Beetle! the drone of Thy dolorous note

Be ever the trance of this tremendous throat!
I await the awakening! The summons on high,
From the Lord Adonai, from the Lord Adonai!

Regarding *Adonai*, the title given to the Holy Guardian Angel, we could pay some little attention to the very last verse in *Liber LXV* as having some further bearing on this task of exegesis. It says: 'And my lord Adonai is about me on all sides, like a thunderbolt, like a pylon, like a serpent, and like a phallus, and in the midst thereof he is like the woman that jetteth out the milk of the stars from her paps, yea, the milk of the stars from her paps.'

It may sound ludicrous and most obscure until we commence the task of elucidation using our basic Qabalistic tools.

A =	*Aleph*	= thunderbolt by shape and by attribution.
D =	*Daleth*	= literally a gate; thus a pylon.
N =	*Nun*	= literally a fish, attributed to Scorpio, one of whose triune meanings is the serpent.
I =	*Yod*	= finger of the hand; even in Freudian terms it is the symbol of the phallus.

Thus, the first part of the term simply explicates and emphasizes that the Lord *Adonai* surrounds one on all sides. One is altogether enclosed within his divinity. The woman who jettith forth the milk of the stars from her breasts is of course Nuit, the Lady of the Starry Heavens, the Egyptian symbol of Infinite Space, within which the nebulae appear, and thus cognate with *Ain Soph*. The *Adonai* is a spiritual centre within the boundlessness of the Infinite Light, and in a sense symbolized the infinite God to the finite natural man.

Further about the serpent: for example, Hans Jonas in his authoritative text *The Gnostic Religion*, had this to say:

> More than one gnostic sect derived its name from the cult of the serpent ('Ophites' from the Greek *ophis*" 'Naasenes' from the Hebrew *nahas*–the group as a whole being termed 'ophitic') and this position of the serpent is based on a bold allegorizing of the biblical text...The Peratae, sweeping consistent, did not even shrink from regarding the historical Jesus as a particular incarnation of the 'general serpent', i.e., the serpent from Paradise understood as a principle... By Mani's time (third century) the gnostic interpretation of the Paradise story and Jesus' connection with it had become so firmly established that he could simply put Jesus in the place of the serpent with no mention of the latter.

There are some interesting possibilities here, for the Hebrew there is a word *nachosh*, a serpent. Analysing the word as before, we obtain:

N = *Nun* = Scorpio = Serpent = 50
Ch = *Cheth* = Cancer = The Chariot in Tarot = 8
Sh = *Shin* = Fire = The Holy Spirit = 300

The total enumeration is 358.

Now we must consult *Sepher Sephiroth* once more. There we find under the same number another Hebrew word *Meschiach*, translated as the Messiah, the annointed one:

M = *Mem* = Water = The Hanged Man in Tarot = 40
Sh = *Shin* = Fire = The Holy Spirit = 300
Y = *Yod* = Virgo = The Hermit in Tarot = 10
Ch = *Cheth* = Cancer = The Chariot in Tarot = 8

This, too, adds up to 358. Inferentially, therefore, we must deduce that the serpent and the Messiah have much in common. By means of the serpent power, the interior transforming fire of the spirit, the Adept becomes transformed into a Messiah or a Redeemer to his own inner world at the very least, if not in some occult manner to mankind as a whole. Each man who gains freedom thereby renders freedom a greater possibility other men.

Now look at the sequence of ideas in each of these two words. The serpent transforms the Adept into a '*Mercabah* (chariot) - rider' towards his mystical home in the Infinite Light–that is to say, it is the powerful agent involved in his illumination. The second word yields analogous material. By sacrifice of all extraneous factors, the Holy Spirit or the Guardian Angel, acting as the hermit or silent illuminator of mankind, ascends Ezekiel's chariot and moves heavenward.

IAO

Then there is the Gnostic name of God – IAO. It is one of those archaic names of which the so-called *Chaldean Oracles* says: 'Change not the barbarous names of evocation for they have a power ineffable in the sacred rites.' Well may we ask, what kind of power does this name have? This question may be answered by transliterating the name into Hebrew. From there, its Yetziratic attributions will provide a degree of enlightenment. There are two ways of doing this; both are interesting.

$$\left. \begin{array}{l} I = \textit{Yod} = \text{Virgo} = 10 \\ A = \textit{Aleph} = \text{Air} = 1 \\ O = \textit{Vau} = \text{Taurus} = 6 \end{array} \right\} = 17$$

Seventeen represents the number of squares in the swastika or Fylfot Cross. By shape it represents *Aleph*, the thunderbolt. And *Aleph* is the first letter of the alphabet, and is 1.

$$\left.\begin{array}{l} I = \textit{Yod} = \text{Virgo} = 10 \\ A = \textit{Aleph} = \text{Air} = 1 \\ O = \textit{Ayin} = \text{Capricorn} = 70 \end{array}\right\} = 17$$

81 is a mystic number of the moon. Luna is attributed to *Yesod*, the Foundation. Its number is 9. The magical square of Luna is 9 x 9, giving 81 squares. This does not fit into our discussion in the least, so the previous method is more appropriate.

If the numerical value of IAO, then, is 17, referred to *Aleph* and so the thunderbolt, by the symbolism described above, we have a much clearer idea of the divine power involved. It is that of the Father of all the Gods wielding the thunderbolt (the Scandinavian swastika or the Tibetan *dorje*) to further his intent of creation. Furthermore, notice that we have *Aleph*, the thunderbolt acting in the divine Air, sandwiched between two earthly signs, Virgo and Taurus, whirling their substance into the appropriate function of creation.

What a long way we have gone from 'Jesus of Nazareth, King of the Jews'. And if our Qabalistic methods will enable us to gain this much insight from merely four letters, it can be left to the student to gather to what lengths we can go to become enlightened on the basis of other words and other ideas. They will show how vast are the possibilities involved in but a single word or sentence. The English translation of the *Zohar* presents innumerable examples of exegesis of many simple biblical notions. Before you know where you are you have been swept away on an exciting wave of spiritual adventure that can only end with the melting of the soul in its divine source.

To conclude this essay, I am going to select one or two more examples, which are fairly complex in substance and import, in order to demonstrate how some of these Qabalistic modes of exegesis work. This particular example is from *The Vision and The Voice, Liber 418*, second part of the Fourteenth Aethyr (Equinox V, Supplement:)

> The blackness gathers about, so thick, so clinging, so penetrating, so oppressive, that all the other darkness that I haver ever conceived would be like bright light beside it.
>
> His voice comes in a whisper: O thou that art master of the fifty gates of Understanding, is not my mother a black woman? O thou that art master of the Pentagram, is not the egg of spirit a black egg? Here abideth terror, and the blind ache of the Soul, and lo! even I, who am the sole light, a spark shut up, stand in the sign of Apophis and Typhon.
>
> I am the snake that devoureth the spirit of man with the lust of light. I am the sightless storm in the night that wrappeth the world about with desolation. Chaos is my name, and thick darkness. Know thou that the darkness of the earth is ruddy, and the darkness of the air is grey, but the darkness of the soul is utter blackness.
>
> The egg of spirit is a basilisk egg, and the gates of the understanding are fifty, that is the sign of the Scorpion. The pillars about the neophyte are crowned in flame, and the vault of the Adepts is lighted by the Rose. And in the abyss is the eye of the hawk. But upon the great sea shall the Master of the Temple find neither star nor moon.

EXEGETICAL ANALYSIS

This whole speech is one of crossing the abyss and the visionary entry into the *Sephirah* of *Binah*, the third emanation on The Tree of Life. It is attributed to the Great Sea, from which all life has emerged, to the planet Saturn which is the planet of death as well as of stability. It is further attributed to *Aimah Elohim*, the mother of the Gods and to Isis as well, the goddess of Nature, to Babalon who is the goddess representing Shakti, which is the universal creative energy and joy, amongst many other meanings. With these basic clues, much of what is cryptically stated in the vision becomes relatively clear.

Since the vision opens with blackness, this becomes a fundamental declaration that the seer is on the right track. All the symbols are harmonious, and the association pathways are not cluttered with inappropriate symbols.

Binah is translated as 'understanding'. And since attributed to Saturn and death, a related symbol would be Scorpio which is attributed to the Tarot card 'Death', usually meaning involuntary change, transformation, sublimation. The *Sepher Yetzirah* letter relative to Scorpio is *Nun*, which means a fish, and its number is 50. These are the gates of understanding, fifty in number, all links in a long but valid chain of associations. Scorpio is also the basilisk. Saturn is black, the colour of mourning. Since Isis, the great Mother, is attributed to this sphere, we have the statement, 'Is not my mother a black woman?' And, as we have learned earlier, the sign of Apophis and Typhon is the sign of destruction.

To each of the five points of the Pentagram is attributed one of the five elements. The five-pointed signet star is in the shape of the perfected man who has developed all phases of his personality represented by the elements. Each of the latter has its own symbols. In the Eastern system, spirit, the quintessence or *Akasa*, is represented by an upstanding black egg.

Binah is also represented by the correspondence of night, the darkest blackest kind of night which Crowley at one time poetically represented by the City of the Pyramids under the N.O.X. or Night of Pan, and at times by the name of a former lady friend Leila, which he promptly transliterated into Hebrew–thus *Laylah*, meaning Night. In this way he transformed a personal relationship into a symbol of a high spiritual experience. These attributions are all referred to *Binah* and *Shekinah*–the divine Presence of the immanence of God, and to Chaos, the realm of the unformed and uncreated.

The vision as a whole, therefore, related to *Binah* and Scorpio, to death and rebirth, to the transformation of the ego-ridden man into NEMO, 'no man', because by dying to self, he has become identified with the Holy Spirit of all that lives, the Self.

THE FAMA FRATERNITATIS

One of the old Rosicrucian classics previously mentioned is the *Fama Fraternitatis*. It was first published at Cassel, Germany, and of course circulated freely amongst mystics, alchemists and occultists of the time in Europe. An unabridged version of the *Fama*, together with some of the other Rosicrucian classics, is to be found in an excellent book entitled *Rosicrucian Fundamentals* (New York, 1923) by Khei° (the late George Winslow Plummer) of the Societas Rosicruciana in America. In Arthur Edward Waite's book *The Brotherhood of the Rosy Cross* (University Press, New York, circa 1963) an edited version is to be found.

The *Fama* purports to give the history of the founder of the Rosicrucian Order, one Brother C.R.C. or Christian Rosencreutz, said to have been born in 1378. His education and travels are delineated at some length. Parts of this dramatic history were extrapolated for inclusion into the Adeptus Minor ritual of the Golden Dawn. A great deal of Qabalistic exegesis has been undertaken on the basis of this history by various members of the Order at different times. Perhaps the most readily accessible is *The True and Invisible Rosicrucian* order written by Paul Foster Case. This latter book goes into such extraordinary detail and analysis of the minutiae of the *Fama* and other early Rosicrucian documents that perhaps the beginner is likely to be overwhelmed by the great wealth and skill of exposition demonstrated by the author. The more advanced student will see in it a useful source book upon which he can build, by this own ever-expanding knowledge of the methods depicted here and by his own meditations.

I select one or two names from the *Fama* to indicate how they can be elucidated by means of the Qabalah of number and symbol. For example, the story narrates that C.R.C. made a bargain with the Arabians to take him to Damcar. Some of the early commentators have suggested that this was Damascus. But since the legend is symbolic these names need to be interpreted symbolically.

If we transliterate Damcar into Hebrew, following our previous rules, we have two words: *dam* (*Daleth* and *Mem*), which means blood, and car (*Caph* and *Resh*), a word meaning lamb. Our name place, then, becomes transformed into a symbol of the 'Blood of the Lamb'. Of course the Rosicrucians were Christians, and Christians of the Reformation; but being mystics they interpreted the traditional Christian body of knowledge in a symbolic manner. So 'The blood of the Lamb which taketh away the sins of the world' of necessity was taken symbolically by them.

The Lamb is *Agni* in the Hindu Scriptures, symbol of the sacrificial fire, and of course in the West it is Christ. As indicated in the essay on meditation, it is hypothesized that meditation accompanied by other occult work succeeds in altering the chemistry of the blood, which in turn changes the normal function of the cerebral cortex. The result of this is that, with the cessation of cerebral or cortical activity, illumination can occur. That is to say, the ego is eclipsed and the Adept for the time being becomes, or realizes, he is a vehicle for the divine spirit, the Lamb of God.

The temple at Damcar where C.R.C. was taken by the Arabs, who at that time were the repositors of the ancient knowledge, is thus the Adept himself, his own organism. For are we not told that the body is the Temple of the Holy Ghost? Thus it is implied that the Arabs who took him to Damcar initiated him into some of the secrets of practical occultism so that he became a vehicle for the transmission of the forces of the higher spiritual planes.

But let us look at the Gematria of these two words:

$$Dam = Daleth + Mem \quad \text{and} \quad Car = Caph + Resh$$
$$4 + 40 = 44 \qquad\qquad 20 + 200 = 220$$

We can take the words separately and then together. For example, *dam* (44) which means blood, equates with words for a ram (*telah*) and flame (*lehat*) and sorrow (*agam*). These words are taken from *Sephir Sephiroth*, which has several words tabulated under specific numbers. Some little meditation by the student will enable him to integrate these words together under the aegis of the primary exegetical meaning of 'The Blood of the Lamb'.

The word *car* (220), meaning lamb, equates with *Baher* (the Elect) as well as one of the Old Testament words *nephilim* (meaning giants). The student should not experience much difficulty in relating these words with our basic term.

On the other hand, if we take Damcar with the number 264, we find in *Sepher Sephiroth* words like *chekokim*, meaning hollow or cavities, and *rehotim* meaning channels, troughs, or pipes. These two latter words were originally used in connection with the ten *Sephiroth* of The Tree of Life, implying that they were cavities or channels through which flowed *Mezla*, the divine life and spirit.

One final manipulation reveals a little bit more. $2 + 6 + 4 = 12$. This number was dealt with on an earlier page in connection with the path of Gimel, the High Priestess of the Tarot. All of these words and numbers and symbols are descriptive of Damcar, and meditation will enlarge the concept still further.

CONCLUSION

These are some of the approaches taken by the Qabalists of many schools, ancient and modern, Hebrew and Christian, orthodox as well as what G.S. Scholem has mistakenly called nihilistic mysticism. Some of these methods may appear to be strained and arbitrary. Perhaps they are. At the same time, however, should they elicit even a shred of meaning from otherwise obscure texts, and illuminate the darkness of sterile scriptures that some feel may be important, then we can take the simple point of view that they have served a useful purpose.